HUSTLE

TO WEALTH

HOW I TURNED A GIG JOB INTO A FORTUNE

CHARLES WEST

Published in 2024 by Staten House

Book design by Mark Wainwright
Cover design by Michelle Lloyds

ISBN - Paperback: 979-8-89686-273-4

Staten House

I dedicate this book to the memory of my parents and to all the vibrant residents of Liverpool, Manchester, and Chester who rely on taxis for their everyday journeys.

HUSTLE
TO WEALTH

AN UNCOMMON GUIDE TO
FINANCIAL FREEDOM

Charles West

Contents

CHARLES WESTS' DISCLAIMER

Please note that while this book discusses various aspects of professional taxi driving including my own busy schedule, it is imperative to state that driving excessively long hours without adequate sleep, rest, or maintaining good physical and mental health is hazardous. It is crucial for everyone, especially those in professions that require prolonged periods of driving, to prioritise their well-being and safety. Prolonged periods of wakefulness can impair judgment and reaction times, similar to the effects of intoxication, and thus, should not be undertaken. Always adhere to the recommended hours of service regulations and prioritise your health to ensure not only your own safety but also the safety of others on the road.

Preface

Welcome to my story that's a bit like a movie except it's all real, a journey from a boring office in London to freedom on the open roads, and eventually, to finding success in ways I never imagined. This isn't just a story about changing jobs. It's about discovering new paths to happiness and success that I didn't even know existed.

Back in 2014, I was stuck in a job that looked good on paper but felt terrible in real life. I worked in finance in London, a city where everything is expensive, and I was supposed to be happy with my good salary and fancy job title. But I wasn't. Despite making £40,000 a year, I was drowning in debt, unhappy, and felt trapped. I owed £28,000 in council tax and credit card debt and lived in a tiny room, struggling to make ends meet.

Then, something changed. I decided to become a taxi driver, a choice that many people might see as a step down. But for me, it was a step towards freedom. This book is about that choice and what came after. It's about how driving a taxi and later, investing in property and index funds, turned my life around.

I want to make it clear from the start that when I talk about driving a taxi or working with Uber in this book, I mean the same thing. It's all about the lessons I learned and the people I met along the way, no matter the name of the service.

There's more to this story than just driving around the city. I also figured out a simple but powerful way to make money through property and index funds. I started small, with what little I could save, and slowly but surely built a property portfolio worth more than £1 million in under 8 years. And the best part? I managed to climb out of £28,000 of debt to get there.

This book isn't just my story. It's a guide to show you, step by step, how I did it. It's for anyone feeling stuck or thinking they're trapped by their life choices. If you're dreaming of a way out but scared of what that might mean, this book is for you. I'll take you through my journey, from the depths of debt and despair to freedom, financial stability, and success.

While self-help classics like "Think and Grow Rich" by Napoleon Hill, "The 7 Habits of Highly Effective People" by Stephen R. Covey, and "Rich Dad Poor Dad" by Robert Kiyosaki offer valuable advice on self-improvement and motivation, they often fall short on providing concrete guidance on wealth-building. These books may inspire a mindset shift or increased effectiveness, but they lack a step-by-step approach to financial growth, such as detailed investment or business startup instructions.

This is where this book stands out. In this book, I not only inspire but also provide readers with a comprehensive, step-by-step guide on transforming their lives. Offering practical advice and the necessary inspiration to take control of their futures. My message is clear: it's never too late to alter your course, and sometimes, the unconventional path leads to the most fulfilling destinations. Whether you find yourself stuck in your current situation, yearning for financial independence, or simply seeking an inspiring tale of transformation and triumph, my journey is bound to motivate and empower you to take meaningful steps toward a more rewarding life.

Anyone, whether they are tradesmen such as plumbers, electricians, tilers, plasterers, or business owners, can follow the strategies outlined in this book to gain financial freedom by dedicating more time to their work. Let's start this journey together, and I'll show you how taking the road less traveled can lead to places you never thought possible.

Chapter 1

How I Escaped My 9 to 5 Job

In 2014, I was stuck in a very boring and stressful finance job at one of the biggest banks in London. It was supposed to be a prestigious job with a fancy title at the middle office of an investment bank, but it was nothing like what I had imagined. Every time I saw an advert on TV asking if I hated

Mondays, I would nod in agreement, because I dreaded going back to work after the weekend.

My boss was a tyrant who tolerated no mistakes or delays. Everyone in the team hated him, but we were too afraid to speak up. He would call you in his office and grill you for coming even a minute late, or for missing a deadline by a fraction of a second. He would also take the credit for any good job you did, and never give you any recognition or appreciation. He would always find faults and flaws in your work, and never give you any feedback or guidance. He would also keep you out of the loop of any important decisions or projects, and make you feel like you were dispensable and replaceable.

We were contracted to work from nine to five, but we often ended up working from nine to eight each day, and from nine to midnight at the end of the month. We had no work-life balance, no time for ourselves, our families, or our friends. We had no bonuses, no incentives, no rewards, no benefits, no perks. We had only stress, pressure, anxiety, and frustration.

I hated my job with a passion. I hated going to work, I hated sitting in a cubicle, I hated looking at a computer screen all day, working on spreadsheets and reports that seemed meaningless and repetitive. Finance was not what I had learned at university, where I had studied economics and accounting with enthusiasm and curiosity. These days, in finance, you are just like an administrator or a clerk, doing mundane tasks and following orders.

After five years of this soul-crushing job, I had had enough. I started looking for an exit strategy, another job that would give me more satisfaction and freedom. But it was not easy to find one, especially in London, where the cost of living was sky-high and the competition was fierce. At the time, I was basically living a hand-to-mouth life, from paycheck to paycheck, even though I had a good salary of £40,000 a year. But in London, that wouldn't get you too far. I was living in a shoebox-sized room, paying about £700 a month, and I was constantly being chased by bailiffs.

I owed about £5,000 in council tax, and I also had about £18,000 in credit card debt. I had accumulated these debts over the years, trying to keep up with the lifestyle of my colleagues and friends, who seemed to have more money and more fun than me. I also had a CCJ against my name, which meant I couldn't take out any new credit card or loan, or even open a bank account.

At that time, I was also overweight and unhealthy. I was comfort eating, binging on junk food and alcohol to cope with the stress and depression. My girlfriend also left me, because she couldn't stand my constant complaints and worries about my life situation. She said I was too negative and pessimistic, and that I needed to change my attitude and my habits.

I felt like I had hit rock bottom, and I didn't know how to get out of it. I had often used taxis to go from place to place, but I never thought of becoming a taxi driver myself. It was when my close friend, who used to work as a carer in a local hospital, transitioned to become a taxi driver, that he started telling me about the taxi business. But still, I wasn't interested. I still had the archaic idea that being a taxi driver was a lowly job for the less fortunate. Even though I could clearly see that my friend had more time on his hands to spend with his family, and that he had a brilliant work-life balance compared to my miserable existence.

What got me to start paying attention and make me start researching the taxi business was when I saw a documentary on TV about *the billion-dollar taxi driver*. A man called Sudhir Ruparelia. He was a humble taxi driver who had worked hard as a taxi driver in London, and then moved to Uganda, where he started up many businesses, including banks, hospitals, and breweries. He was now a billionaire and a philanthropist, helping his community and his country. He said that being a taxi driver had taught him many valuable skills and lessons, such as customer service, communication, negotiation, problem solving, and entrepreneurship.

That documentary inspired me and made me curious. I started doing the maths, and I realised that being a taxi driver could be quite lucrative. I calculated that if a taxi driver could do a £10 trip in about 10 minutes, that meant he could probably make £30 to £40 an hour. That meant he could make on average £150 to £300 a day, depending on the demand and the traffic. As I later found out, there were a lot of drivers making this kind of money, and some were even making more. So I was hooked, and I decided to sign up as a taxi driver.

That was the best decision I ever made in my life. Before becoming a taxi driver I had tried an failed in starting an Amazon and an Ebay business. I also tried gambling but gave up after just two months as I thought no one had ever gotten rich from gambling except there were exceptionally lucky. Becoming a taxi driver changed everything for me. It gave me a new perspective, a new purpose, and a new passion. It also gave me more freedom, more flexibility, and more money. I was able to pay off my debts, improve my health, and enjoy my life. I also met a lot of interesting people, and learned a lot of things. I discovered new places, new cultures, and new opportunities. I became a successful taxi driver, and I never looked back.

Chapter 2

Signing up to become a taxi driver

So, why become a taxi driver? The big advantage is flexibility - the ability to work on your own terms. But remember, it's a business, not just a side gig. Before you even pick up your first passenger, there's a lot to do.

How to Become a Taxi Driver in London

In London, you'll need to start with a Transport for London (TfL) application, costing around £650-£700. This includes your application fee and the license once you're approved. You can apply online or by mail, but online is faster.

Next up, you need an Enhanced DBS check to ensure your background is clear. It costs about £50 and takes a week or so. Once you have the DBS reference number, you can proceed with your TfL application.

A medical exam, usually done by your GP, is also necessary. It costs around £80. With these steps completed, your application needs to be submitted to TfL and then you have to wait a few months. It took me about six months from start to finish.

You will also have to take the topographical test. It involves using a computer, a mouse, and an *A to Z Master Atlas* of Greater London. The test includes identifying locations and plotting routes on a map. It's more about computer skills than geography.

If you have any medical conditions, like sleep apnea, TfL might ask for additional information. Make sure your condition is under control and doesn't affect your driving ability.

Once you pass all these steps and get your TfL license, you're almost ready. Next, you need specific private hire insurance, which is pricier than standard insurance. Shop around for the best deal. Despite having a 7-year no claims discount and a regular car insurance cost of £400, my initial insurance premium was £3000. Make sure that when you get insurance, it includes a licensed courtesy taxi car so you can continue working in case you get into an accident.

Your vehicle also needs a TfL MOT, and its compliance is signaled by a disc displayed on your windscreen. The next step is to choose your platform – local taxi company, Uber, Ola, Bolt, etc. The onboarding process varies, but generally, you'll need to submit various documents and sometimes attend training or an in-person verification. I started with Uber and a local london taxi firm then later I signed up with Ola and bolt.

Payment schedules differ among platforms, and remember, some show the gross fare, while others show the net amount after their cut. It is important to be on all of these platforms. Treating this as a business is crucial. Invest in two good phones and a reliable used car - more on cars in another chapter.

How to Become a Taxi Driver in Liverpool

First, you'll need to visit your local council and sign up for a taxi driver training course. This course costs about £200-£250 and it covers important topics like discrimination, disability awareness and how to treat your passengers. It's a 3-day course and quite insightful.

You will also need a medical check, which can set you back £50 - £80, and an eye test for about £10 - £20. Then, there's a local council test. I got my license from Sefton council and their test consisted of a few easy questions such as how much change you would have to give back to your passenger if they gave you £10 and the fare was £8.75.

Once you've completed these steps, your council will issue your personal private hire driving license. This lets you drive any vehicle registered with your council.

As for the costs, you're looking at about £300-400 in total. This includes the training, medical exam, optician's fee, and the private hire driving license(badge) fee, which is around £30-£40 per year.

The whole process might take 3-6 months, considering you have to wait for your medical and optician appointments and complete the training course.

So, to kickstart your journey as a taxi driver in Liverpool, your best bet is to chat with your local council. They'll guide you through all the necessary steps.

How to Become an Taxi Driver in New York City

First things first, you need a TLC (Taxi and Limousine Commission) license. This is a must-have for all ride-share drivers in NYC. The process starts with an application that you can fill out on the TLC website. There's a fee involved, so be prepared for that.

Before you apply, though, there are a few prerequisites. You'll need to complete a 24-hour TLC Driver Education Course and pass the associated exam. This course covers everything from navigating NYC streets to understanding TLC rules and regulations.

Next up, you'll need a physical exam. It's pretty straightforward and ensures you're fit to drive. After that, you'll have to pass a drugs test.

Now, the fun part - the DMV (Department of Motor Vehicles) test. You've got to pass a written exam that covers driving rules and regulations in New York. It's a bit tricky, but with some study, you'll get through it.

Once you've ticked all these boxes, submit your TLC application with all the required documents, including proof of your completed course and exam, your physical exam results, and your drug test clearance.

The waiting game begins once you've submitted your application. It can take a few weeks to a couple of months for TLC to process everything. When you finally get your TLC license, the next step is to find a suitable vehicle.

In NYC, your car needs to meet specific requirements set by Uber and TLC. It should be in good condition, relatively new, and comfortable for passengers.

You'll also need commercial vehicle insurance and the vehicle must pass the TLC inspection. This inspection is more rigorous than your standard DMV test, focusing on the safety and comfort of the vehicle.

With your TLC license and an approved vehicle, you're ready to apply to Uber or Lyft. The application process is pretty straightforward. You upload your documents, including your TLC license, insurance, and vehicle inspection report. Once Uber approves your application, you can start driving.

Chapter 3

FINDING THE IDEAL CAR FOR YOUR TAXI BUSINESS

Do not buy a new car as it can be financially damaging

Many people just love a new car smell as they think it smells like power and freedom but actually, the smell is just petroleum based solvents evaporating off vinyl and plastic. I doubt if many people will still like that new car smell if they find out what it's really costing them.

Since the auto boom of the 1950s, cars have become an integral part of society. Car companies spend billions in advertising each year and their advertising budget keeps rising. They convince us that once we are behind the wheel of a new car, our families will love us more, our neighbors will envy us, and our freedom to go anywhere is secure. Unfortunately, a new car is more likely to take away your freedom and security. New cars are a financial triple threat. You borrow money at interest to buy an asset that you have to pay to maintain and and which drastically depreciates in value. Cars retain their value about as well as ice cream on a hot day. A new car will depreciate 63% in the first five years. 10% of that the moment you drive it off the lot. Calling cars a "bad investment" is is like criticising a cat for its lackluster skills in software development. They are not an investment at all. Can you think of anything except new cars that you would spend much money on that loses value quickly?

Also leasing a car is not a good idea as leasing companies set their prices so that you pay for the depreciation of their vehicle, and when it's over, they still have an asset they can re-sell. So let's set a few simple ground rules that will put you in the driver's seat instead of being taken for a ride. Number One, buy a car that's at least 5 years old. Right away, you're skipping the majority of its depreciation. Number Two, save up to buy a car in cash. Paying interest on something that loses value is like gaining weight from exercising. All pain but no gain. Number Three, If you can't comfortably afford to save an amount equal to your car payment, you can't afford it. So if you're not saving £300 a month, you shouldn't take on a £300 car payment.

So how much money is actually at stake if we run the numbers? Let's say you buy a new car for £20,000 and you put £4,000 down as deposit then you finance the rest over 60 months at 4.25%. Your monthly payment will be £295.42. That sounds pretty normal. But check this out. What if you bought that same car, but a 5-year-old model, which costs you 63% less or £7,400 in this case. Put your same £4,000 down as deposit, and with the same loan arrangement, you're looking at a payment of just £62.78 per month. That's a monthly saving of £232.65.

Now you could take those monthly savings of £232.65 and put them into a growing asset, like a home or an index fund. And if you continued to do that for 35 years at a very conservative 7% per year return, you would have over £421,459. That could be enough to retire on for some people. So that's just one thing you can start doing now to prepare for your future. There are many more as I will explain in chapter 8 and 9.

Similarly because of the high upfront costs I have never considered using electric or hybrid vehicles for Taxi. Although these vehicles are cheaper to operate, the savings might not compensate for the higher purchase price. The availability of charging stations is inconsistent, and the limited range of electric cars can cause anxiety about running out of power, leading to potential operational challenges for me as a taxi driver. Maintenance costs for hybrid and electric vehicles can be higher due to specialised parts and fewer qualified repair shops. This can result in longer downtimes and lost income for taxi drivers who depend on their vehicle's reliability. I recently watched a YouTube video in which a couple were quoted $60000 to replace an electric car battery when the car as a whole costs less than $60000.

So I strongly urge you not to buy or use a new car for Uber, Lyft or any taxi services. You don't want to rack up miles on a new car that has not yet depreciated, as depreciation could be one of the largest expenses for a taxi driver. You might not see the cost directly coming out of your account, but it impacts you financially in the long run. For example, if you buy a car for £30,000 to £40,000, drive for Uber, and put on 50,000 miles, you might make £20,000. However, your car's value could depreciate by £20,000, essentially netting you zero pounds. Not to mention, you're likely going to make a loss due to fuel, maintenance costs plus your insurance will be higher compared to if your car is used. In Chapter 9, I talk about how you can use the concept of the time value of money to invest your cash wisely, aiming for a better return instead of splurging it on a new car.

Consider opting for a used car instead of splurging on a brand-new one. Take my experience, for instance—I've been driving a 2014 Skoda Rapid 1.2 TSI since 2017. When I bought it, the car had already clocked 140,000 miles. Over the years, I drove it up to 450,000 miles before deciding to swap out the engine. I found a used engine on eBay for £900, and it only had 60,000 miles on it. Remember, a car is essentially the sum of its parts, unlike a human body that might reject an organ transplant. With some tuning, you can make a used car outperform a new one. Take a cue from movies like Fast and Furious—Vin Diesel and his crew aren't out buying brand-new cars to upgrade. Even veteran black cab drivers, with over 30 years in the taxi business, swear by the reliability of used cars. That's why you still see black cabs over 20 years old still in service. The saying "when in Rome, do as the Romans do" applies here—don't be swayed by flashy advertisements, and don't spend your hard-earned money on a new car.

Many drivers believe that purchasing a used car results in hefty maintenance expenses. However, if you buy the right used car, you won't find yourself shelling out much for repair bills. In my experience, the most expensive repair I've encountered was an engine replacement. I bought a used engine for £900 and paid an additional £600 for the installation. This major repair occurred only once in the four years I've owned the car, prompted by a minor oil leak.

My annual car maintenance costs typically include brake pads, amounting to £68 once a year, and servicing every six months, involving the replacement of spark plugs, oil, and air filters, costing around £100. I've learned to handle these tasks myself by watching instructional videos on YouTube. If you decide to perform your own car servicing, be sure to invest in the correct safety equipment. Not only does this save money, but it also spares you the time you'd spend waiting for a mechanic's appointment. Beyond brake pads and servicing, my only other yearly expenses involve suspension drop links and shock absorbers, totaling £200, with an additional £100 for labour cost. For a well-maintained used car, you should expect to spend between £500 to £1000 at most on annual repairs and maintenance.

Here are some tips for buying a used car. Consider ebay, craigslist, gumtree and Facebook Marketplace which is honestly the best option if you take all precautions against scammers. However, if you know nothing about cars, it might be more challenging. I recommend for taxi you should use only petrol engine versions of Toyota, Honda, Skoda, VW or Seat. Go for manual gear box if you are in Europe. Avoid Hyundai, Chevrolet, Kia, fiat, Peugeot or Renault. Also avoid luxury brands like BMW, Saturn, Mercedes, Pontiac, Infiniti whose parts can be expensive and hard to find. Failure to get a Toyota, Honda, Skoda, VW or Seat you can go for a Ford Fusion in the USA or Ford Mondeo in the UK. This is the only car in the Ford range which has stood the test of time.

When you find a car on Facebook Marketplace or a similar platform, message the seller. Ask if you can take the car to a mechanic for a brief inspection. A trustworthy seller should have no issue with this. Do not pay any deposit for a car you find on Facebook Marketplace as usually it is a scam if the seller asks for a deposit upfront before you have even seen the car. Buying a car from a private seller can save thousands by avoiding dealership markups. So avoid dealerships where possible, as you will likely end up paying over the odds.

Always, use leverage when buying a car. Leverage, in this context, means having something the seller doesn't - in this case, time. Don't appear desperate instead, show that you can wait for the right deal. On Facebook Marketplace, start by offering below the asking price and negotiate from there. People often need to sell quickly, and if you're not in a rush, you have the upper hand. If a car is listed for £7500, always start with £5000.

How to spot a car scam on facebook marketplace

Have you ever scrolled through Facebook Marketplace, eyes sparkling at the sight of that perfect car, only to wonder, "Is this deal too good to be true?" In our digital age, the convenience of online shopping comes with its own set of challenges, especially when it comes to buying cars. Here are some steps to help you spot those sneaky car scams on Facebook Marketplace.

1. The Price Tag: Too Good to Be True?

Let's start with the most obvious red flag, the price. Extremely low prices can be a lure used by scammers to grab your attention. Do a quick comparison with similar models and their average market prices. If the deal sounds like a once-in-a-lifetime opportunity, proceed with caution.

2. The Pressure Cooker Salesman

Scammers often create a sense of urgency. They might say something like, "This offer is only valid for today!" or "You won't find a deal like this anywhere else!" Remember, buying a car is a significant investment, and it should never be rushed. Any seller pushing you to make a quick decision should set off alarm bells.

3. Mysterious or Overly Enthusiastic Sellers

When interacting with the seller, pay attention to their responses. A legitimate seller will likely know a lot about the car they're selling and will answer your questions in detail. If you encounter vague responses, reluctance to provide detailed information, or an eagerness to sell without proper discussion, be wary.

4. The Vanishing Act: No Physical Viewing or Test Drive

Always insist on a physical viewing and a test drive. If the seller constantly makes excuses to avoid this, it's a huge red flag. No matter how genuine the photos look, seeing the car in person and taking it for a spin is non-negotiable.

5. Suspicious Payment Requests

Be cautious if a seller asks for payment through unusual methods like wire transfers or gift cards. These payment methods are a scammer's dream because they're hard to trace and almost impossible to refund. A genuine seller will usually agree to more standard payment methods. And never pay a deposit so the car can be placed on hold for you.

6. Title Troubles

Always ask to see the vehicle's documents like a log book before making a purchase. Make sure the name on the title matches the seller's name. If they're selling the car for a 'friend' or the title isn't in their name, it's time to walk away. You don't want to be stuck with a car that can't be legally transferred to you.

7. The Storytelling Seller

Some scammers use emotional stories to win your trust and sympathy, like claiming they're selling the car because they're moving abroad urgently. While these stories could be true, they're often used to manipulate potential buyers. Always focus on the car and the transaction.

8. The Request for Personal Information

If a seller is more interested in your personal details than selling the car, it's a red flag. Never share personal information like your National Insurance or Social Security number or bank details with someone you've just met online.

Facebook Marketplace can be a treasure trove of great deals, it's crucial to stay alert and cautious. Always check from third party websites like HPI if there is any outstanding finance on a car you want to buy. Trust your instincts – if something feels off, it probably is. Remember, it's better to miss out on a deal than to fall victim to a scam.

Should you lease a car?

I recommended buying a used car with cash as the most financially sensible option. Or putting down a deposit of at least 70% but for some people, this may not be possible. The majority of people in the UK and the USA finance their vehicles with loans, and with rising prices and rising interest rates car loans are getting more expensive than ever. The average interest rate on a new car has gone from 4.4% to 7% in just a few years. Britain's car market heavily relies on financing. Approximately nine out of ten of the 2.3 million new cars sold in a typical year are paid for using some form of financing provided by financial institutions. As a result the amount that people in the UK owe on cars is fast rising to unsustainable levels. In the USA the amount that Americans owe on cars has doubled since 2011, making up over 9% of total US consumer debt. You would think that this might be a good time to forego buying and lease a car instead since with a car lease there is no debt, no commitment, and lower monthly payments than a car loan. Car leasing can seem attractive at first, but lease agreements have plenty of financial pitfalls, and are just as vulnerable to price and interest rate hikes as buying. They are not always a bad idea. Ultimately, it depends on what matters to you, and how much you're willing to pay for it. The fundamental misconception about car leases is that they work like other rental agreements, like for apartments or furniture. They don't. Cars are a unique asset because they depreciate very quickly. Nothing costs so much yet loses value so fast as a car and lease agreements are designed to account for depreciation. Here's how it works. If you wanted to lease a new car for the typical term of 36 months, the dealer will take the selling price of the vehicle and subtract what it's predicted to be worth in three years, known as the residual. The result is essentially the depreciation, how much value the car will lose while it's in your possession, which you are required to pay off in monthly instalments. The bad news is the depreciation is treated like a debt. Just like a car loan, you'll pay interest and fees determined by your credit score, and often be required to put up a down payment. In this way, a car lease is less of a rental, and more like buying the most expensive years of a car's life. And because they depreciate so quickly, that can be close to half its total value. True, it's less than the sticker price so your monthly payments are lower than a car loan would be for an equivalent vehicle, but when the lease is up, you have no asset to show for it. Some lease agreements allow you to buy the car at the end of the term at its residual price, but because leases tend to have higher fees than car loans, you'll end up paying more than if you had just bought it outright to begin with. Another supposed advantage of leasing a car is the freedom it affords. For those who are scared of commitment, it can seem exciting to swap vehicles every few years, but leasing comes with its own set of restrictions. First of all, most lease agreements have a mileage limit for the term of the lease, usually between 12,000 and 15,000 miles per year. So you must confirm this if you plan to use the car as a taxi because a taxi driver will do anywhere from 25000 to 100000 miles a year. If you go over the mileage limit on a car lease contract, you'll pay extra at a rate as high as 50 pence per mile. You can opt for a higher mileage limit, for a higher monthly payment of course, and you will not be reimbursed for any miles you didn't use.

When you lease a car you must return the car exactly how you received it. So don't bother upgrading the stereo, or installing custom rims, unless you don't mind reinstalling the old ones before you take the car back. And lastly, lease agreements are notoriously hard to get out of. Early termination incurs penalties that are sometimes as much as the total remaining balance all at once. And unlike car owners, you can't just sell the vehicle if you don't want it anymore. You're pretty much stuck with it until the term is over. To be fair, there are some advantages to leasing a car. Many lease agreements include routine maintenance costs, and newer cars are typically still under a manufacturer's warranty. That's no small thing, considering car repairs are one of the most common unexpected financial crises people have to deal with. You'll never have to go through the hassle of selling it. And if you own a small business, leasing a car can offer big tax benefits. Unlike car loans, in which you can only deduct the interest, lease payments by businesses whether taxi or not are fully tax deductible.

Personally, I believe the primary attraction of car leasing is mostly psychological; having access to a nice, new, reliable car that you otherwise wouldn't be able to afford. The benefits of comfort, status, and safety may not be financial, but that doesn't mean they're worthless. Some might think what is the point of money if it can't make us happy? But still I am of the opinion that car leases are not worth enough to justify the cost. Assume two people Michael and Dave are both in the market for a car, and each has room in their budget for around £500 to £600 a month, with the same good credit score. Dave decides to buy a new car for £20,000. He puts £3,000 down, and ends up with 36 monthly payments of about £540. Michael wants something fancier, so he decides to lease a new car with a selling price of £40,000, which will lose about 40% of its value over the three year term. He also puts down £3,000, and including interest and fees, he'll end up paying about £580 a month for 36 months. At the end of three years, both men have paid roughly the same amount of money, but their financial situation couldn't be more different.

Dave now owns his car free and clear, and he can sell it for probably half to two thirds of what he paid for it, or he can drive it until it falls apart, which could be five to 10 years from now, depending on how well he cares for it. Michael, on the other hand, is right back where he started. Instead of buying out the residual for £24,000, he opts to lease another new car under the same terms. If we fast forward another three years, Michael would have paid about £25,000 more than Dave. After a total of nine years, even if Dave has had to shell out £10,000 in maintenance and repairs, he'll still be almost £40,000 ahead of Michael. Michael isn't paying that money for nothing. He gets to cruise around town in a brand new ride with all the amenities. Whether that's worth it depends on what matters to him. But generally speaking, if you can't afford to buy a basic new car, you probably can't afford to drop £40,000 on a luxury car either. At the end of the day, inflation and rising interest rates haven't changed the maths on leasing.

If you have a car in working order, take good care of it, and drive it for as long as you can. And if you're in the market for a vehicle, buying, even with a car loan, still makes the most financial sense. Leasing provides the short-term benefit of driving a nicer car for lower payments, but you're not solving a problem, you are just buying time. Even if Dave had picked a £20,000 car, after 10 years, he would have ended up paying a bit more than Michael. The main problem for a taxi driver is that car leases in the UK often limit you to driving 8,000 miles a year. But a taxi driver usually drives between 25,000 to 100,000 miles a year, so leasing a car for your taxi business in the UK is not an option.

Why you should not buy a car from a dealership

First reason is they just charge too much money for their vehicles. The guys that sell cars at a dealership are professionals. They do it for a living so they would try to squeeze all possible profits out of the car. They have no personal involvement in the deal as it's just a used car they are selling. Generally their Commission is the percentage of the sales, the higher the price the more money goes into their pocket. Usually cars being sold at dealerships will go anywhere from two to four times what the dealership actually paid for the vehicle. Being professional car salespeople, if they got a car they know sells well, they will wait until they get as much as they possibly can. If you are buying from a private individual they would probably be in a hurry to get money.

oore, many dealerships offer expensive extended warranty packages which many people never use. And if they tried to use it they usually can't because of some fine print in the terms and conditions which people always miss. A friend of mine experienced an engine failure, and when they attempted to utilise their warranty, the warranty company stated that the engine was already damaged when the car was purchased, and they don't cover pre-existing conditions.

The best thing to do when buying a used car if you are not good with cars is to have a mechanic check out the car before you buy it. That's the best insurance, because warranty policies are not going to cover all kinds of repairs. Usually when a warranty policy refuses to pay for a repair it is difficult arguing with a big insurance company.

Another reason not to buy from a dealership is, a lot of them have these cars they claim are certified used cars or approved used cars. Usually these are certified by the dealers themselves just so they could charge more for the cars.

One of the most significant benefit for buying a used car from a private seller is the opportunity for price negotiation. Private sellers are often more flexible and willing to negotiate the price directly with the buyer. This flexibility can stem from their desire to sell the car quickly, the absence of overhead costs that dealerships face, or simply because they've already found a new car and need to make space. As a result, buyers may find that they can purchase a vehicle at a lower price than what is typically offered at dealerships. Additionally, since numerous private sellers lack extensive knowledge about cars, they might be eager to sell their vehicles due to what they perceive as a significant issue, even if it's minor. Consequently, fantastic deals can be found in the real world, but they're less likely to be discovered at dealerships.

Another reason to consider purchasing from a private seller is the level of transparency and insight into the car's history. Private sellers are likely to have a complete record of the vehicle's maintenance, repairs, and any issues it may have encountered. They can share firsthand experiences about the car's performance, reliability, and quirks. This personal connection to the vehicle can provide a buyer with a clearer understanding of what they are purchasing, as opposed to the more generic history reports a dealership might provide.

Furthermore, buying a car from a private individual can often lead to a quicker and less bureaucratic transaction process. Dealerships are notorious for lengthy paperwork, upselling additional services, and including hidden fees that can make the buying process more complicated and costly. In contrast, transactions with private sellers are typically straightforward, focusing solely on the exchange of the vehicle and payment. This simplicity can make the entire process less daunting and more efficient for both parties involved.

Why you should not buy a used car at auction

Purchasing a used car at an auction might seem like an opportunity to land a great deal, but it comes with significant risks that potential buyers need to be aware of. One of the primary concerns is the limited access to the vehicle's history, making it difficult to assess past accidents, maintenance issues, or other hidden problems. Additionally, cars sold at auction are often offered "as-is," meaning there's no warranty or guarantee of condition, leaving buyers with little recourse if problems arise post-purchase. The inability to test drive before buying further compounds the risk, preventing buyers from identifying potential issues with the car's performance and condition.

The competitive nature of auctions can also lead to inflated prices, sometimes resulting in buyers paying close to or above market value for a vehicle. This, coupled with the excitement of the bidding process, can lead to overspending and buyer's remorse. Moreover, the initial cost of the car is just the beginning, with auction fees, registration, taxes, and any necessary repairs adding to the total investment. These hidden costs can quickly turn what appeared to be a bargain into a costly venture.

Most cars are at an auction for a reason, and it's not a good reason as many of them are wrecked, flooded, stolen, or repossessed cars by banks and needless to say, those cars have not been taken care of very well and they may have been written off by an insurance company.

With the price of modern new cars being sky-high, many people are looking for a good used vehicle so a good car doesn't need to go to an auction because there's plenty of people waiting to buy it. In 2012 I bought a citroen c4 picasso from auction. The outside looked perfect but after I bought it I realised the electronic parking brake was not working. After trying several mechanics who could not repair it I took the car to a Citroen dealership who quoted £3800 for the repair. I had bought the car at auction for just £1800. I eventually sold the car to a mechanic for £1200.

Even when you are at the actual car auction in person, you don't get much of a chance to check a car out, you can't have a road test or use the scan tools to see if anything's wrong.

Usually when a car drives in at an auction and the professional car dealers start bidding it is because they know how to buy cars at auction as they have people who will repair the car for them. Buying at auction is a skill that I have honed with properties as I have spent a few years buying at property auctions like I explain in chapter 8. For cars it is not my expertise and usually car manufacturers will put in technology which only them can repair so you keep coming back to give them money.

The case against renting a car for taxi

Renting a car for taxi purposes might seem like a straightforward option at first glance, but when you crunch the numbers, it doesn't make much financial sense. Let's break it down. Imagine you're renting a car for £200 a week. Over five years, that's going to add up to a whopping £52,000. Now, if you were to buy a decent used car for £7,000 instead, and let's say your insurance is around £3,000 a year, with maintenance costs about £1,000 annually, you're looking at spending roughly £27,000 over the same period. That means you could be saving an impressive £25,000 after five years. And that's assuming the worst-case scenario for insurance and repair costs.

I've been in the taxi business, and I've seen firsthand how these costs play out. When I started, my insurance was £3,000 a year, but it's since dropped to £1,000. My repair bills, mainly for things like shock absorbers, brake pads, and general servicing, are usually around £400 a year. Sure, I've had a few pricey repairs here and there—like the time I had to shell out £700 for a new clutch or £1,500 for a new engine. But even with those unexpected costs, buying still comes out on top financially compared to renting. Plus, there's something to be said for the peace of mind and flexibility you get from owning your car outright. The feeling of starting each week without owing money to a rental company is priceless.

Why you should buy a Toyota, Honda, VW, Skoda or Seat

To start, these cars can remarkably reach and exceed 300,000 miles. They showcase highly reliable engines with robust drivetrains, ensuring dependable performance. Not only do these vehicles come equipped with excellent alloy wheels, mirrors, straightforward handles, and easily reachable tail lights accessible through the trunk, but they are also cost-effective to repair. The key to their enduring lifespan lies in their uncomplicated maintenance and affordable replacement parts. These cars are designed with user-friendliness in mind when it comes to servicing. Features such as convenient access to the battery, airbox, and vital components like brake fluid and fuses simplify the maintenance process. The engines benefit from a timing chain, contributing to their longevity, and facilitate easy access to spark plugs, ignition coils, fuel injectors, and even the oxygen sensor. Furthermore, the EGR valve, crucial for emissions control, is both easily accessible and budget-friendly to replace.

While some manufacturers innovate at the cost of reliability, others, like Honda and Toyota, prioritise durability and longevity. The engines in these cars are not just about power; they are about enduring performance and dependability. So, when considering your next vehicle, remember that the best engines are those that combine performance with reliability, ensuring a smooth and worry-free driving experience for years to come.

There is a story of a man in Australia who's Toyota clocked more than 1 million miles. When you look at videos from developing countries pay attention to the kind of cars they use for their taxi - these are mostly Toyotas because they are reliable even on bad roads. If you tune in to Scotty Kilmer's YouTube channel, you'll discover that Toyota is his preferred car brand.

Uncomplicated and sturdy design defines Toyotas, Hondas, VWs, and Seats. These cars assure longevity, reaching hundreds of thousands of miles with simple oil services and regular coolant flushes. Opting for the petrol version with a manual gearbox is advisable, especially if you're in Europe.

How to check used cars before buying

Almost all modern cars are computerised these days, so having an OBD2 reader is a game changer. It's a universal fit for any car from 1996 onwards. If you don't have one, consider investing in one – some are as affordable as £40. I got mine for £45. Plug it in to any car you want to buy and make sure there are zero diagnostic trouble codes. If there are no codes, it could mean the car's in good shape, or the codes were recently cleared. Check the readiness test to see how long it's been since the last reset.

Next up, park on a flat surface and look for any oil leaks. Then jack up the front end and take a closer look underneath. Check the CV joints to ensure they are intact. Then check the engine and transmission for any leaks. While the car is jacked up, give the tires a tug to check for any suspension issues.

Make sure you go to view the car in daylight. Good sunlight is your best friend for comparing panels and spotting any paint jobs. A fresh coat might mean the car's had an accident or is hiding some rust. And if one panel's rusty, chances are others are too, and that's a big red flag. Check the car body for damage, which could indicate past accidents or flooding.

Under the hood, check the transmission fluid. Make sure it is a nice red fluid that's not low, and give it a sniff to make sure it doesn't smell burnt. Then check the engine oil – it should be clear and not smell funky. However, keep in mind that oil can be changed before selling, so it's not always the best indicator of a car's health. Check the engine for any signs of leaks or corrosion and inspect the oil's condition. Belts and hoses should be free from cracks and wear, and all fluid levels must be adequate, as their condition can significantly impact the car's performance and longevity.

Close the hood and check the alignment; the seams should be even on both sides. Do the same for all door seams. Make sure they all match up. Next, open the boot. Check for any signs of rear end collisions. Then take a good look at the paint job. Check the reflections for any dings or scratches.

Moving inside the vehicle, the condition of the interior can tell you a lot about how the car was maintained by its previous owner. Test all electronic components, including the dashboard lights, to ensure everything is working as it should. Also, be aware of any unusual odours, as they may indicate problems like water leaks or mechanical issues.

Don't forget the tires. You want them to be flat and evenly worn. When inspecting the tires, turn them all the way to one side and run your hands over them to feel for even wear. Uneven wear could signal alignment issues or past accidents.

Then check the brakes. You can gauge the wear by looking at the brake fluid reservoir. If it's low, your brakes might be worn down. But remember, the reservoir could have been topped up.

Now, the general condition of the car is important. Check for corrosion and rust on exhaust and aluminium parts, and make sure the antifreeze looks clean, without any oil mixed in.

And, of course, take the car for a test drive. A good 10 minutes in town and 10 miles on the highway. Listen for any odd noises and pay attention to how the car handles, especially at higher speeds. Turn off the radio and listen for any odd noises. Noises can be warning signs of costly future repairs. And don't let the seller distract you during the test drive. Keep your ears open and focus on the car. After the test drive check again for any leaks.

If you're serious about buying, it's wise to get a professional mechanic to do a final inspection. It's worth spending a bit on an expert check-up when you're about to save thousands on a used car.

Before making your final decision, do some online research. Check if it has any outstanding finance on it or if it has been in an accident before which was recorded by the insurers. Check out what other owners say about the car. Remember, for every negative review, there are probably hundreds of happy drivers who just aren't posting about it. And if the car is for your taxi business make sure it is a petrol version of a Toyota, Honda, VW, Skoda or Seat.

Chapter 4

Potential earnings as a taxi driver

I began my taxi-driving career by working for both a local London taxi company and Uber. I was excited to have left my boring office job and I was no longer a cubicle slave. But I quickly realised that I wasn't making much more money than before. Every week, I earned about £700, but after paying off my huge credit card bills and taxi expenses, I was just getting by, paycheck to paycheck. Even worse, I kept getting chased by bailiffs for unpaid council tax, parking fines and unpaid rents from a previous house. I tried moving to different places to avoid them, but they always found where I lived. I didn't know that every time I did a credit check in order to get a new phone or buy something with credit, it updated my new address for anyone, like the bailiffs, to see. So, even though I was hoping for a fresh start with my taxi job, I ended up in the same tough spot, struggling with money. I was struggling for money but my mental health was great as I was no longer a cubicle slave.

I had my first *eureka moment* occurred when I had a ride with an elderly gentleman named Ryan. A former special forces soldier turned nurse and later a lawyer who now owns three law firms. In our conversation, he casually mentioned that he exercises everyday and he only sleeps 3.5 hours a night and puts in a staggering 18 hours of work each day. That revelation hit me hard. When I got home that day, I looked at myself in the mirror and got upset about my own laziness. At 34, I realized I couldn't keep up with a 63-year-old man. I was also dealing with being overweight at 186 lbs and having insulin resistance, which made me tired after big meals. That got me thinking, and the very next day, I decided to step up my game by working more hours.

I started earning £1000 weekly which I was proud of. Then my Kia ceed which I had maxed out my credit card to buy for £5000 broke down. After hitting a pothole, the automatic gearbox of the car began leaking oil and eventually ceased functioning. Frustrated with this issue and having decided that I had had enough of Kia vehicles, I opted to sell the car for spare parts and advertised it online. Then I had a second *eureka moment* when a Russian guy who used to be a taxi driver in London came to buy the car as he was now in the business of buying cars that need fixing and shipping them to Russia. As I was talking to him he told me he used to earn £1500 a week working as a taxi driver in london. Then he explained to me his work schedule and I decided to copy and perfect it. Going forward I would ask Uber drivers and black cab drivers what they were earning. That is how I found out some London black cab drivers were earning as much as £200k a year. That would mean they are technically out earning the prime minister who at the time was on £152k a year.

The earning potential of an Uber driver varies depending on several factors such as location, hours worked, type of car and driving times. As a rule of thumb you should not be earning less than £1000 a week before expenses while working 40 hours in a week in a city with a population of around 500,000 people. Talking to drivers in New York I found out that in New York doing 30 hours a week should make you $80000 dollars a year. So 60 hours a week in New York should get you $160000 in a year.

During my one-year stint as an Uber driver in London, most drivers I spoke to were making £1200 a week, with a few earning £1600. Motivated by this and inspired by the Russian man who came to buy my car, I stepped up my game and began averaging £1800 a week. While there were weeks with higher and lower earnings, my average was consistently £1800 during the period I committed myself to the work. Subsequently, due to the high cost of living in London, I made the decision to move to Liverpool. The world is vast, yet many people confine themselves to a small spot; I was determined not to be one of them. In Liverpool, my average weekly earnings, before expenses, stood at £1550 for a solid six years. Excluding the downtime caused by the COVID-19 pandemic, my average earnings remained around £1550 per week.

If you're online looking up what people think about driving for Uber as a job, you'll see all sorts of negative opinions. But here's the thing, a lot of the negative comments and videos come from YouTubers or bloggers who aren't even doing Uber driving full-time. It's pretty important to keep that in mind.

Some youtubers complain and say Uber driving is not a good career option and that you will earn less than the minimum wage. Morgan Housel in his book *The psychology of money* brilliantly explains that this type of pessimistic viewpoint often sounds more intelligent and can be more seductive than optimism. If you have 10 people praising Uber as a career and one person criticising Uber, the majority of people will believe the person criticising Uber because human beings are risk averse in their nature. One question to the pessimists is why do you see all these expensive cars being used as taxis if there is no money to be made? I have seen someone using a Range Rover for Uber taxi business.

The bottom line is if you master your craft you will become successful. If you are lazy as an Uber driver like I was when I started then you are not going to make any money in the taxi business and you will spend time complaining on the internet. Making money with Uber involves both working smart and hard. You have to treat your work as a taxi driver as a business. Numerous businesses fail to survive beyond the initial few months, similarly, a significant number of Uber drivers quit within the first few months of starting. To be successful you have to first get the right car and make sure that most of the money you earn stays with you.

If you're thinking of working as an Uber driver or doing any form of taxi driving all day, every day, it is not going to be a walk in the park. Imagine being behind the wheel for 10 hours a day, every single day of the week, it's tough. You are going to feel like Tom Hardy being chased in the movie Mad Max Fury Road. But after a while, you get used to it. Your body adjusts to being in the driver's seat for long, and driving gets easier.

To make decent money with Uber you have to both put in the hours and work smartly. The person who came up with the quote 'work smart and not hard' has never been in the taxi business. The car you choose is very important. You want something that doesn't consume fuel like there's no tomorrow and won't break down every other week. Picking the right car means you spend less on upkeep and fuel, and more of the money you make actually stays in your pocket. Make sure you get a petrol version of a 5 doors Toyota, Honda, VW, Skoda or Seat with a manual gearbox if you are in Europe. Ensure the engine size is below 2L. I used a Skoda Rapid 1.2 TSI.

I have a preference for manual gearboxes. This stems from my experience with a mechanic, a gentleman from Afghanistan based in Manchester, who owns a small taxi rental business. When I had to replace my engine, I rented a Skoda Octavia from him for a week. Even though I wanted an automatic Skoda Octavia at first, he told me that all his cars with automatic gearboxes needed fixing because the gearboxes were broken. He also advised against using an automatic car for taxi services, especially if I intended to cover extensive mileage. Also, in my early days as a taxi driver, I had to sell my Kia Ceed for spare parts due to a malfunctioning automatic gearbox. During my time using the Kia Ceed for Uber, its suspension components required replacement every 3 or 4 months, along with a steering rack replacement at one point. In contrast, with the Skoda, the only suspension part that needed changing annually was the shock absorbers.

To make the most money from the taxi business you have to figure out the best times to drive in your city. You've got to learn when and where people need rides the most. Is it during the morning rush hour? Weekend nights? Maybe when there's a big concert or a sports event in town? Driving during these busy times will really bump up your earnings. Don't forget, it's not just about driving around. There's the time you spend waiting for ride requests, taking care of your car, and being friendly and professional with passengers – that matters a lot as a good rating from passengers will lead to more tips.

Being a full-time taxi or Uber driver has its ups and downs. It takes a mix of working hard, being clever about how you work, and being able to tactically deal with angry passengers. Usually there are very few angry passengers especially with Uber as Uber customers know Uber has their details in case they need to be tracked down. If you are ready to put in the hard work with your taxi business then you will get a handsome reward out of it.

My work schedule

In London, the average earnings for Uber drivers range from £150 to £200 from Monday to Thursday, and then increase to between £250 and £400 per day from Friday to Sunday, based on the hours they opt to work. Personally, my daily earnings during the weekdays were between £200 and £280, and on weekends, specifically Friday, Saturday, and Sunday, I earned between £300 and £500. In Liverpool, my earnings were slightly lower, with £180 to £250 from Monday to Thursday and £300 to £450 on weekend days. Sometimes, on special occasions such as Valentine's day or St. Patrick's Day, which is widely celebrated in Liverpool due to its large Irish community, I can make over £500. In both London and Liverpool, I used to work from 2 am to 9 am and then from 3 pm to 10 pm.

Notice that my schedule covers all the peak periods — when children and employees are commuting to and from school and their workplaces and when people are going out for nightlife and returning. I stuck to this routine diligently for the 7 years I worked as a taxi driver in Liverpool, mainly driving for Uber. Here's a breakdown: I'd do a 30-minute workout at 9:30 am, then grab a meal and take a 3.5-hour nap until 2:30 pm. After that, I'd start my first work shift from 3 pm to 10 pm, followed by sleep from 10:30 pm to 2 am. Then I would do my second shift from 2:30 am till 9:30 am.

I religiously followed this schedule for 7 years, except on event days like concerts, football games, or horse races. It's important to note that sticking to my schedule wasn't a walk in the park, which is why I conditioned myself like an endurance athlete would. Every day, I made sure to exercise for 30 minutes, meditate for 10 minutes (usually while waiting for a ride request), and stuck to a slow carb diet from Monday to Thursday, as recommended in Tim Ferris's book "The 4-Hour Body." On weekends, I switched to a keto diet. Keep in mind that everyone's body is different; for me, this was the only diet that allowed me to keep going for 14 hours a day, split into two 7-hour shifts.

Creating a schedule involves thoughtful planning at the start of each week. Typically, I plan out my week on Mondays. I begin by determining the number of hours I intend to work (usually 14 hours a day) and assess whether I need to adjust my schedule due to any events happening that week.

Staying alert: becoming Uberman

Working 14 hours every day is no small feat. Driving for long hours, especially at night, can be risky if you're not fully alert. My holy grail strategy for staying sharp is what I call "micro-dosing" on sleep or meditation. Micro-dosing on sleep involves napping for anywhere between 3 minutes to 15 minutes – these are what I refer to as micro-sleeps. When I'm driving and feel tired, I find a spot to park and take a quick 3-minute micro-sleep, and if needed, I may extend it to 6 minutes, or even take a 15-minute nap later on.

Although 3 minutes may seem short, it's surprisingly effective. Personally, a micro-sleep works better for me than any coffee, energy drink, or caffeine tablet on the market. Before discovering micro-sleep, I tried various methods. While exploring ways to stay alert, I checked out popular taxi driver forums on Reddit, but aside from suggestions like coffee and energy drinks, some advice was either odd or illegal. Some even recommended using drugs like crystal meth or engaging in masturbation when feeling tired. Then, I stumbled upon Tim Ferris's book, "The 4-Hour Body," where he talks about the Uberman sleep pattern and how you can reduce nightly sleep by incorporating a series of daily naps. Inspired by this, I developed my own sleep cycle, sleeping 7 hours a day in two 3.5-hour shifts. I've been following this sleep pattern for 7 years now without any health concerns.

Scientists know little about why we humans spend one-third of our lives asleep while bigger animals like the giraffes sleep for just under 2 hours a day. Is there any reason why humans can't emulate giraffes? Sleeping for 2 hours a day means we spend 22 hours being awake. With this extra time, think of the adventures we could get up to. This would open up a new world of possibilities. Thomas Edison, the famous inventor of the light bulb and motion picture camera, slept very little each night, only about 4 to 5 hours, because he wanted to work more. He thought sleeping less would make him more productive. Instead of one long sleep, he took short naps throughout the day. Taking short naps through out the day is called polyphasic sleeping while sleeping for 7 to 9 hours in one block is called monophasic sleeping. Today, scientists say most people need 7 to 9 hours of sleep to be healthy and think clearly, so Edison's way of sleeping isn't recommended for everyone. The best approach to sleep and being a taxi driver is to develop what works for you as an individual.

Another great hack for staying alert while driving is eating raw nuts or seeds (my preferred being raw groundnuts and raw pumpkin seeds). Consuming them slowly one at a time can serve as an effective strategy for maintaining alertness and energy levels while driving. This approach not only provides a healthy snack option but also contributes to sustained digestion in the stomach, which keeps you alert. Nuts, being a rich source of healthy fats and proteins, may help support sustained energy levels and enhance cognitive performance. By incorporating this mindful snacking habit during driving, you can promote digestive well-being, potentially reducing the likelihood of fatigue and enhancing overall alertness on the road.

Staying Fit Behind the Wheel

Taxi drivers spend a lot of their time sitting down, which can lead to health problems if they're not careful. It's important for them to stay active to keep their bodies healthy.

Aerobic exercise, like walking, running, or cycling, is great for the heart. It makes the heart stronger and more efficient at pumping blood around the body. This can help reduce the risk of heart disease, which is important for taxi drivers who sit for long periods. It also helps with weight control and boosts mood, making long days behind the wheel a bit easier to handle.

Strength training is another good choice. It involves using weights or your own body weight to build muscle. For taxi drivers, strong muscles can make everyday tasks easier and protect against back pain, a common problem from sitting all day. It also helps with controlling blood sugar levels, important for avoiding diabetes, and keeps bones strong.

Yoga is perfect for stretching and flexibility, which can help prevent stiffness and pain from sitting in the same position for too long. It's also great for stress relief. Driving can be stressful, dealing with traffic and passengers. Yoga helps to calm the mind, reduce anxiety, and improve focus, making driving safer and more enjoyable.

My personal exercise routine

After finishing work each day at 9:30 am, I would dive into a 30-minute workout routine. It involved 10 minutes of walking (not running) on my home treadmill, followed by 15 minutes of strength training with 15kg dumbbells, and wrapping up with 5 minutes of yoga. I'd usually find a yoga video on YouTube and follow along. I got my treadmill and dumbbells from Facebook Marketplace for a total of £70.

I intentionally avoided intense aerobic exercises every day because they tend to wear me out, making it challenging to wake up for my next shift. That's why I stuck to walking on the treadmill instead of running.

Events to look out for in order to maximise earnings

As a taxi driver, there are numerous opportunities to boost your earnings by keeping an eye out for specific events. Here are a few examples:

Major Sporting Events: Major sporting events such as football, rugby or horse racing can be a great opportunity for taxi drivers to earn extra money. During these events, there is usually a high demand for transportation services, and operators like Uber charge higher rates. During horse racing events such as Aintree and Chester race days, I typically earn a minimum of £300 due to the high demand from visitors coming in from out of town.

I am a big football fan; I support four teams; Liverpool FC, Manchester United, Manchester City and Evertoon as they all make me a lot of money each year especially when they win which means their fans will stay out longer thus needing taxis to go home after the buses and trains have stopped working. Each day Manchester United, Manchester City, Liverpool or Everton play at home I would usually make £350 and above. My passengers are always surprised and perplexed when I reveal my support for these four teams. Then I would take the opportunity to explain that it is all business to me just like football which is also a business where players can be paid to play for any team. However, they often struggle to comprehend why one person would back four teams, especially when they are rivals.

Usually when any of the Manchester teams are playing I go and work in Manchester. Whenever I work in Manchester I sleep in my car, so I always carry a sleeping bag, hot water bottle and a flask with hot water during the winter.

Concerts and Festivals: Concerts and festivals are another great opportunity for taxi drivers to earn extra money. During these events, there is usually a high demand for transportation services, and Uber usually charges higher fares. You need to make sure you are checking all the concert venues in your city for any upcoming events.

Holidays: Holidays such as Christmas, New Year's Eve, and Valentine's Day are also great opportunities for taxi drivers to earn extra money. During these holidays, people tend to go out more, and there is usually a high demand for transportation services.

Airport Runs: Airport runs are a great way to earn extra money as a taxi driver. Many people need transportation to and from the airport, and operators like Uber usually charge higher rates for airport runs. Airports are consistent hotspots for taxi services. While competition might be higher, the demand for airport pickups and drop-offs is steady. Offering services like pre-booked rides and ensuring punctuality and reliability can help in building a regular clientele for airport runs.

Nightlife: Nightlife areas such as bars and clubs are also great places to find customers as a taxi driver. Many people who go out at night need transportation services, and you can charge higher rates for these services. You want to have the city centre or major bars and clubs as your rides waiting points.

Tourist Seasons and Hotspots: Tourist seasons bring a significant influx of visitors needing transportation.

Familiarity with popular tourist destinations, hotels, and routes can give taxi drivers an edge.

Weather-Related Opportunities: Unpleasant weather conditions often lead to increased demand for taxis. During heavy rain, snow, or extreme weather events, people prefer taking taxis over walking or using public transport. Keeping an eye on the weather forecast and positioning oneself in busy areas during these times can lead to a higher volume of rides.

Pay dates for students and workers: Usually month ends are busy as most jobs pay at month end but there are days which get busy unexpectedly such as days where students get their student grants if you live near a university and when shift workers get paid if you live near something like an amazon factory. As a master of your craft you want to get into the student media and learn when the big events and pay dates are.

What types of rides make the most money while online

When I started working for Uber in 2014, taking long trips was the better option as they would pay you extra if traffic made you take long to get to the destination. However now the best option is to take the short trips as you would earn more and you would spend less on fuel. As a rule of thumb for me I only take rides which pay at least twice in money value compared to the number of miles for the trip. For example if a trip is 2 miles I need to get at least £4 for the trip. During busy periods I would only take rides paying 3 times or four times the mileage depending on how busy it is. If it is busy, do not accept, for example, a 10-mile trip paying £18, when 2-mile trips are going for £7. By the time you complete the 10-mile trip and return to the city after covering 20 miles and wasting more fuel, another driver taking the 2-mile trips would have done 3 trips, thus making £21 and spending less on fuel.

My strategy to earn the most money is to stay at a radius of 3 miles from the city centre. That is, I do not take passengers going more than 3 miles from the city centre especially when it is busy. I would only take trips longer than 3 miles when I have been waiting for a while without a trip request and I made sure the trip was paying at least twice the mileage amount, so for a 6 miles trip I would demand to get at least £12. When it's busy I would demand at least £18 and at least £24 when it is extremely busy.

Expenses and tax

As a taxi driver, you can typically deduct various expenses related to your taxi business from your taxable income. That is, to calculate your tax, you deduct expenses like fuel from your earnings before you apply the tax rate which is now 20% of earnings after deductions in the UK. However, it's important to remember that tax laws can vary by country and region, so it's always a good idea to consult a tax professional or refer to your local tax authority's guidelines. Generally, the following expenses are commonly deductible for taxi drivers:

Fuel: Costs of gasoline or diesel. Usually fuel costs for the type of vehicles I used were 10 percent of earnings at most. My last car, a Skoda Rapid 1.2 TSI was averaging 9 percent so if I made £300 I would spend at most £27 on fuel. As a rule of thumb any car with less than a 2 litres engine should average 10 percent of earnings for fuel cost. So make sure not to use any car with engine size bigger than 2 litres.

Maintenance and Repairs: With car maintenance you have to be sensible and find a mechanic that would accept to replace your own parts then you can just buy parts from your local dealers or from ebay. To further save costs I learnt how to service my car and change brake pads.

Insurance: When you start off as a taxi driver insurance will be your biggest cost. I started off paying £3000 per year even though I had 7 years no claims discount but then the amount halved after 2 years and in my last year I paid £1000 for my insurance after being a taxi driver for 8 years. Always shop around for the best insurance deal.

Depreciation: Depreciation on the vehicle, if owned.

Lease Payments: If the vehicle is leased, the lease payments may be deductible. I do not recommend leasing a car to use for your taxi business.

Tires: Costs of new tires and maintenance

Licences and Fees: Cost of obtaining a professional driving license or renewing it. Any fees paid for taxi operation permits or regulatory compliance.

Office Expenses: Mobile phones and bills; if used for your taxi business purposes.

Taxi Dispatch Service Fees: Fees paid to taxi dispatch services or ride-hailing apps.

Office Supplies: Logbooks, pens, paper, and other small office supplies.

Health Insurance: If you are self-employed and pay for your health insurance.

Advertising and Marketing: Costs associated with promoting your taxi service, such as business cards, online ads, and local newspaper ads.

Loan Interest: If you have a loan for your taxi vehicle, the interest on that loan is often deductible.

Utilities: If you have a home office, a portion of your home's utilities might be deductible.

Travel Expenses: If you travel to conferences, trade shows, or training related to your taxi business.

Meals and Entertainment: Costs for meals especially during working hours.

Health and Safety Equipment: Costs for items like sanitizers, masks, or gloves, particularly relevant in the context of health guidelines.

Retirement Contributions: Contributions to a qualified retirement plan if you are self-employed.

Education and Training: Costs related to courses or training to improve driving skills or business acumen.

Always keep accurate records and receipts of all your expenses. This is crucial for tax purposes and in case of an audit. Remember, specific tax rules and regulations, including what can be deducted and how, can differ, so it's always a good idea to get advice from a tax professional.

In my situation, each week I would set aside £75 for taxes. During the first year, I got help from an accountant who I paid £200 to file my tax return. After that, I did it myself in the following years because the process stayed the same. The good thing about taxes is you can use the money first and then work hard to pay it in the last month of the financial year. I did this a few times when I didn't have enough money to buy a property, which I'll explain better in Chapter 8. This isn't something you can do if you work for someone else. So, usually, I would spend £140 on fuel to earn £1550. After deducting £75 for taxes and £50 for car maintenance, I'd end up with £1285 per week, totaling £66820 in a year. Normally, in the UK, taxes should be 20 percent of your earnings after deducting expenses. But if you have a creative accountant, they can show you legal ways to reduce your taxes by doing what wealthy people do.

Chapter 5

ROAD TO PERFECTION: EFFECTIVE TIPS FOR TAXI DRIVERS

Driving a taxi can be a great moneymaker, but there are some insider tips you've got to know, whether you're just starting or have been at it for a while. The following taxi driver tips are going to be game-changers for boosting your earnings, skyrocketing your ratings, and just making your driving experience with Lyft, Uber or any other taxi operator a whole lot more enjoyable.

Dash Cam: The more you're out there on the roads, the higher the chances of some kind of altercation. Whether it's a fender bender or some bizarre scenario outside or inside your car, a dash cam is a lifesaver. It's a minuscule investment compared to the costs and headaches of a 'he-said-she-said' situation. Trust me, even if you're not driving for Uber or Lyft, it's an investment worth making.

Don't Move: Wait until your passengers have gotten in or out of your car and shut the doors before you start driving. Some people take longer to get in and out. For example, I once had a group of elderly ladies who were slow to get into my car. Because I was rushing to earn money during a horse racing event, I drove off before they were all inside, and one lady fell to the ground because the door was still open. Luckily she did not sustain any injuries but the incident left me traumatised. I learnt to be patient the hard way.

Peak Hours: This is where the money is so you want to be on the road at peak hours. You should target morning and evening commutes, friday nights, saturday nights. Timings can vary city by city, but generally, you want to make sure you are working during peak hours.

Multiple apps: I dont understand why so many drivers stick to just one app. Signing up for both Uber, Lyft, Bolt or your local taxi firm doesn't cost a penny and can really maximize your earnings. There have been times when one app offers more than the other, and being on both means you get the best of both worlds. Make sure you turn off all other apps when you are doing a job on one app. You can be online on several apps at once, but focus on one ride at a time to avoid complications.

Start Small: To all the new drivers out there, don't go from zero to a hundred real quick. Test the waters part-time, see how it feels, and check the money rolling in (or not). A crucial thing to remember is that location massively impacts your earnings. So, always start small, then decide if you want to ramp it up. For me I made sure I could make an amount I could survive on before quitting my job.

Taxi insurance: It is vital to get a taxi insurance. Let your insurance company know you're driving for Uber or Lyft. You absolutely don't want to find out after an accident that they won't cover you because they didn't know you were using your car as a taxi.

Idling Over Driving: After dropping off a passenger, it's smarter to park safely and wait, rather than drive around aimlessly. You save on petrol, reduce wear and tear, and you're not adding unnecessary miles to your car. The exception is when the city centre is busy and you drop someone miles away from the city centre then you have to drive back to the city centre. So the only place where you should normally park and wait is the city centre.

Caffeine Pills: These will keep you alert without the need to constantly visit the toilet. But, remember, they pack a punch, so check your tolerance level. Also your body becomes immune or resistant to a particular brand after a while so get different brands. Stop immediately if the caffeine pills affects your sleep pattern.

Expenses Tracking: Keep tabs on everything - fuel, meals, miles, car maintenance, even the gear you wear for work. It's all about those tax write-offs when it comes to submitting your tax return.

Phone Mount: This is as important as the dash cam. It's safer, more convenient, and keeps you from missing ride requests. You can find affordable ones everywhere – even at Poundland or dollar stores.

Charging Cables: This is a must-have for both passengers and yourself. Consider getting a multi-charging cord to cater to different phone types.

Say My Name: Remember that iconic scene from 'Breaking Bad'? There's wisdom in there. Always confirm your passenger's name. It's a simple step to ensure you have the right person and adds a layer of safety. Also make sure to check and confirm their destination using the Uber app. I've had instances where passengers entered a location on the app, but upon my arrival, they said it wasn't where they actually wanted to go.

Good Posture: Often overlooked, but long hours of driving can wreak havoc on your back. Consider investing in seat padding or adjusting your seat for better posture.

Huel, Kefir or Slimfast: When you are in a hurry consider Huel, Kefir or Slimfast for food. These are affordable, nutritious, have low sugar and super convenient. These are better than fast food. Also I like to drink water with a bit of baking soda instead of energy drinks or coffee as with energy drinks your energy levels rise and then crash after a few hours but with baking soda your energy levels stay constant.

Early Drop Off: In busy situations like events or heavy traffic, offer to drop passengers off a bit early. It's faster for them, and it keeps you moving, ready for your next ride.

Aux Cord: An aux cord is essential for passenger satisfaction. Music preferences can vary, and an aux cord is simpler and quicker than fiddling with Bluetooth connections.

Events: As mentioned in the previous chapter Keep an eye on local events. Concerts, sports games, festivals – these can be goldmines for taxi drivers.

Follow your schedule: It's easy to lose track of goals when you're your own boss. Stick to your schedule religiously and do not try to make a set amount daily as this will demotivate you if you do not achieve that amount or make you to go home early and earn less if you hit your target amount. Sticking to your work schedule keeps you focused and motivated and makes you to earn more especially on busy days.

Don't look: Don't peek at your earnings until your workday is over. When you keep checking how much money you've made on apps like Uber or Lyft, you might decide to stop working sooner than planned, missing out on extra cash you could have made by staying logged in. Also, looking at your earnings while you're still working can make you feel disappointed and less motivated if you see you've made less than you expected. So, keep your focus on your job, and you might end up with a nice surprise at the end of the day!

Premium roadside recovery: This is a lifeline for any driver. The peace of mind and practical help it offers can be invaluable, especially if you find yourself in a pickle on the road.

Finish Strong: Last impressions count when you drop off. Whether it's a simple "Have a great night Dave" or "Good luck with your audition Sophie," leaving passengers with a positive final interaction can boost your ratings.

Warm food: Bringing warm, homemade food in a small flask is a great idea. It's like taking a piece of home with you. This way, you'll have something comforting to eat, making you less likely to want to head home early just because you're hungry for a home-cooked meal. Plus, it can save you money and help you eat healthier, too!

Gas Guru: Use apps like Gas guru to find the best fuel prices near you. Even modest savings per litre can accumulate to big savings.

Eco Mode: If your car has eco mode make sure you use it all the time. It is a simple feature that can save you a surprising amount in petrol expenses.

4 AM Shifts: Not for everyone, but an early start can mean lucrative airport rides and less competition on the road. My schedule was 3pm to 10pm then 2am to 9am. 2 shifts a day which cover all the busy periods.

Bathroom Addresses: It sounds funny, but knowing where to find accessible bathrooms in the city can be a lifesaver. Bonus tip: invest in a portable urine bottle in case you cannot find a bathroom.

Track your analytics: Monitor when and where you're making the most money. Every city is different, and the more you understand your specific market, the more you can maximise your earnings.

Know Your Costs: Understanding your car's running costs is crucial. This includes fuel consumption, maintenance, tires, etc. It's all about knowing if you're actually making a profit, breaking even, or even losing money.

Selective Acceptance: You don't have to accept every ride. Be strategic and choose trips that make sense for you, whether it's about the destination or the fare.

Don't Chase Surge: Learn the patterns of regular surges in your area instead of chasing random surges, which can be a wild goose chase.

Surge Hacking: Stay on the outskirts of surge areas to avoid heavy traffic and grab those £5 surges instead of getting stuck in traffic for a £15-£20 surge.

Get a Second Phone: This allows you to run your Uber and Lyft apps separately from your personal phone, which is useful for controlling music and other functions. Also, make sure your phone's screen is bright enough at night. This will help you see trip requests clearly without straining your eyes or distracting you from driving.

Adhere to the Law: As a taxi driver, you're not exempt from traffic laws. Always adhere to local regulations.

Sign Up for Everything Uber Offers: From rideshare to Uber Eats to package delivery – having more options means more opportunities to earn.

Chat or Chill: Read your passenger. If they're up for a chat, engage and enjoy the conversation. If not, let them relax in peace. It's all about striking the right balance.

Manage Lost Items: Always check your car for left-behind items at the end of each trip to avoid the hassle of returns.

Master the Uber App: It's complex but essential to know the Uber app inside out.

Dress to Impress: Think business casual. Ditch the sweats and hoodies. Opt for neat jeans or, even better, some classy slacks with a button-up or collared shirt. It's all about giving off that professional vibe.

Clean Ride, Happy Riders: Keep your car spotless. Trust me, a clean car makes a world of difference. A regular trip through the car wash works wonders. I learned the hard way that a dirty car can mean fewer tips. A clean, shiny car just feels more luxurious. And, if you're clocking in a full day, take a break around the halfway mark for a quick clean-up. It makes a world of difference in how passengers perceive you and can directly impact your ratings.

Brush: Keep a brush handy in your car to quickly brush off any crumbs or rubbish left behind in your car by your passengers after each ride.

Freshen Up: Invest in some car air fresheners. They're cheap but mighty effective. Especially if you're juggling UberEats, you want your car smelling fresh, not like last night's dinner. I prefer using California Scents car air freshener with the cherry scent. It makes my car smell like a cherry cake fresh out of the oven.

Be Accommodating: Be responsive to your passenger's needs. Whether it's adjusting the temperature, playing their favourite tunes, or simply offering a mint, these gestures go a long way.

Mini toolkit: Another handy item, especially as taxi driving racks up many miles, a mini toolkit is essential. You never know when something might loosen up or break, so being able to handle minor repairs on the fly can be a lifesaver. Also sometimes a bulb not working might just be fixed by removing and re-attaching the battery terminals as I found out. On several occasions during my night shifts, the police have stopped me and requested that I head home until my rear lights are functional again. However, I always manage to surprise them by whipping out my mini toolkit, replacing the bulbs, and then continuing with my work.

Spare bulbs: Make sure you are always having spare bulbs and learn how to change your car bulbs. This will not only save you time it takes to drive to a fitter but save you being taken off the road by the police or worse fined. You do not want to be taken off the road by the police on a busy night.

Paint touch up: Find out your car's paint code and buy the same color paint from eBay. This way, you can touch up any scratches on your car yourself. Fixing these scratches can help make sure your car passes its inspection and gets its license renewed.

Heated car seat cover: A heated car seat cover is a game-changer during the winter months. It keeps you warm and comfortable, even on the coldest days, by providing direct warmth to your body through the seat. This can help reduce the chill you feel when you first enter the car and can be especially beneficial for those with muscle aches or stiffness, as the heat helps to relax and soothe sore muscles. Using a heated seat cover can also reduce the need to crank up the car's heater, saving on fuel and ensuring the warmth is exactly where you need it most. It transforms your car into a cozy haven, making winter drives something to look forward to.

Spare tyre: It's a good idea to keep an extra tire, a car jack, and a wrench in your car. Also, make sure you know how to change a tire in case it gets flat. You do not want to wait 2 hours for breakdown recovery during a price surge on the uber app. Waiting that long could end up costing you around £80. I can change my car tire in 10 minutes because I learned how by watching videos on YouTube. If I have a flat tire and there's a passenger in my car, I tell them it'll only take 10 minutes for me to fix it or they can choose to get another taxi. They always decide to wait.

Mini vacuum: Make sure you invest in a mini vacuum at home or store it in your car if you have got space. It's great for cleaning up any messes left by riders, like dirt or sand, ensuring your car is ready and clean for the next passenger.

Keep extra fluids in your car: With the amount of driving you do, it's smart to have additional windshield wiper fluid, coolant, and oil on hand for top-ups.

Jumper cables or a **portable jumper battery pack** is essential. If your car battery dies, you'll be thankful you have these to get you moving again.

Puke bags: Trust me, they come in handy, especially if you're driving late at night. They're affordable and can prevent a big mess in your car. Usually I will not pick up any one who is so drunk they cannot walk but if I make a mistake and they jump in I will just hand them a puke bag just to be safe.

Cleaning supplies: It is a good practice to keep cleaning supplies in your car as between rides, you'll want to keep your car spotless for the next passenger. It not only maintains your car's cleanliness but also helps with better ratings and tips.

Organiser: Get a good organiser to keep all your car items neatly stored in your car. It adds to the professional look of your vehicle and ensures everything is easily accessible when needed.

Massage gun: For a taxi driver, spending long hours behind the wheel can lead to muscle stiffness and discomfort. A massage gun can be an invaluable tool in such situations, offering quick relief and promoting relaxation. It works by delivering targeted, rapid pulses to deep muscle tissues, helping to ease tension, enhance circulation, and reduce pain. I usually use my massage gun at home but if you choose to carry it in your car you can use it during breaks or between rides, to address sore spots. A good massage gun will not only alleviate physical stress but also improve overall job satisfaction and performance.

Books: When a taxi driver is waiting for passengers, reading a book is much better for the mind and relaxation than scrolling through social media on a phone. Unlike social media, a book takes you into different stories and ideas, making your mind work and grow. It's a calm and peaceful activity compared to the constant notifications on the phone. Reading a book during the waiting time not only keeps the mind engaged but also helps you to relax and enjoy the downtime. It's like having a good friend in a book that makes the waiting moments more enjoyable and beneficial.

How to increase fuel efficiency

Here are my top tips to get more out of your tank and save money.

Clean Air Filter: A clean air filter improves fuel efficiency by up to 10%. It's super easy to replace your air filter, and there are tons of tutorials on YouTube if you need them.

Check Your Gas Cap: A faulty cap can lead to more oxygen in your tank, making your engine burn more fuel.

Front End Alignment: Make sure your car isn't pulling to one side, which can strain the engine and wear down tires.

Properly Inflate Your Tires: Over 25% of vehicles on the road have the wrong tire pressure. Correct inflation will improve fuel efficiency.

Basic Tune-Up: Tuning up your car with oil changes and changing spark plugs will enhance its efficiency by making the engine run more smoothly.

Reduce Junk in the Trunk: Extra cargo can decrease your fuel economy by 1-2%. Clearing out unnecessary weight will make your car more fuel efficient.

Drive at a Steady Pace: Maintaining a steady pace while driving is a key strategy for enhancing fuel efficiency. It's advisable to refrain from excessive speeding or abrupt stops. By consistently driving at a moderate speed and avoiding aggressive acceleration and braking, you contribute to making your vehicle more fuel-efficient. This not only helps in saving fuel but also promotes a smoother and more economical driving experience.

Only filing up half your tank: Filling your car's tank only halfway can save fuel because it makes the car lighter. A lighter car doesn't have to work as hard to move, so it uses less fuel. Imagine carrying a heavy backpack; it's harder to walk fast, right? It's similar with cars - the heavier they are, the more energy (or fuel) they need to move. So, by not filling the tank all the way, you're making your car a bit lighter and helping it use less fuel on your trips. This will save you some fuel money over time.

Dealing with difficult situations

Driving for Uber or for any taxi operator means you get to meet many people and see new places, but sometimes you might face difficult situations. Here's how to handle them simply:

When passengers are being difficult (like being loud, rude, or drunk), stay calm and remind them to be respectful, following Uber's rules. If they don't listen, it's okay to end the ride safely and tell them their behaviour isn't okay. I usually point to my dashcam and remind them they are being recorded and almost always it diffuses the situation.

Apologise always. Apologising in a road rage situation, even if it's not your fault, can be a wise move for several reasons. First, it helps to de-escalate the tension and can prevent the situation from worsening. Road rage incidents can quickly escalate into dangerous confrontations, posing risks not only to the involved parties but also to other road users. An apology, even a simple one, can act as a peace offering, showing the other person that you're not interested in conflict. This can help to calm tempers and diffuse the situation, making it safer for everyone. Furthermore, prioritising safety and peace over being right in such scenarios demonstrates maturity and emotional intelligence, qualities that are invaluable on the road where cooperation and respect can significantly enhance everyone's safety.

If passengers ask personal questions that make you uncomfortable, politely change the subject or keep the conversation light and professional. In unfamiliar or unsafe areas, trust your feelings. If a place seems unsafe, you can cancel the ride. Use your app to share where you are with friends or family and have a GPS to help with directions.

For disagreements about the route, explain that you're following the GPS for the best route but can change it if they really want to. This helps avoid confusion and keeps the ride smooth.

When there are delays caused by things like traffic, let your passengers know what's happening and apologize for any wait. Keeping them updated helps keep things positive.

In short, stay patient, communicate clearly, and always put your safety first. This way, you can handle tough situations well and make driving for Uber or Lyft a good experience for both you and your passengers.

Just listen

Being a taxi driver often turns the car into a confessional of sorts, where passengers feel the urge to share their most personal stories. If you are friendly and offer a listening ear to those who are up for a chat then you will truly hear some intriguing stories. As a taxi driver, note that you are not a therapist so it is important to just listen and respond if necessary in a caring and non-judgemental manner. It's vital that the person talking to you feels supported and knows they're not alone in their struggle. By listening carefully and showing empathy, you can make a significant difference. It's all about understanding the person's feelings and letting them know that their feelings are valid and heard. As most often people just need a listening ear. Here are snippets from some unexpected discussions I've participated in:

" I have a drug problem and I spend a lot of money on drugs. Even though I make a lot of money it all goes on drugs and my family does not know about it."

"I just lost £3000 at the casino".
Just a quick note: Many people I gave rides to from casinos or horse races had lost money. I gathered this information by consistently asking about their outcomes.

"I just caught my wife cheating with some random guy she met on a night out".

" I am a doctor and I am just from dealing with a situation where a patient had a sex toy lodged in their rectum".

" I took drugs at an event called 'lost' then literally got lost. Some girls found me, kept me at their house till the morning".

" I work as an escort, and tonight was exceptionally rewarding and I got paid well"

" I am a bouncer. I used to be worth 4 million pounds from drug dealing. I got caught, sent to jail and everything got taken off me. Drug dealing is not worth it as I could not sleep in peace".

" I just won £24000 at the Casino and I have ordered for myself a £500 escort for tonight".

"My boyfriend just punched me and he has done it many times before".

"I am a muslim lesbian girl. I told my dad about it, he sent me off for one month of prayers at a prayer camp but then I still remain unchanged. I do not know what to do".

"My son just punched me".

"Can you come back to my house and spoon with me?"

"My boyfriend just broke up with me, can you take me to A&E?"

" I feel like I do not want to live anymore as my wealthy partner left me".

"I've been embezzling money from my company. I started small, but now it's gotten out of control. I'm terrified of getting caught, but I don't know how to stop."

"I'm secretly in love with my best friend."

"I just found out I'm adopted. My whole life feels like a lie. I don't know who I am anymore, or if I should confront my parents about it."

"I'm an artist, but I haven't sold a single piece. I tell everyone I'm doing well, but I'm struggling to make ends meet. Pride won't let me ask for help."

"I've been living a double life. By day, I'm a corporate lawyer, but by night, I perform in a drag show. It's the only time I truly feel alive."

"I accidentally sent a compromising photo to my entire contact list, including my coworkers and family. I don't know how to face anyone now."

"I'm a professional athlete, but I've lost my passion for the sport. I feel trapped because it's all I've ever known, and everyone expects me to keep playing."

"I found a lump in my breast last week. I'm scared it might be cancer, but I haven't told anyone yet. I don't want my family to worry."

"I witnessed a crime, and now I'm being pressured by both the criminals and the police. I feel like I'm in way over my head."

"I'm a teacher, and I've developed feelings for a student. I know it's wrong, and I would never act on it, but I'm struggling with my conscience."

"I hacked into my partner's phone and found messages that suggest they're planning to leave me. I'm devastated but don't know how to bring it up."

"I've been pretending to go to university for the past two years. In reality, I dropped out. My parents are expecting me to graduate next year."

"I faked a degree and got a job as a quantity surveyor, I have done so well and I have been promoted."

" You just saved me from my ex-girlfriend who wanted me to sleep with her even after I had told her I have a new girlfriend."

It is amazing what people will tell you especially when they are drunk.

The free consultations

As a taxi driver, I discovered something amazing. My passengers weren't just people needing a ride; they were like a goldmine of knowledge! I drove all kinds of experts around – doctors, lawyers, accountants, business owners, architects, bettors, athletes, poker pros, and property owners. So, I figured, why not learn from them? Whenever someone felt like chatting, I'd ask for advice. If a doctor hopped in, I'd ask health questions. If a landlord was my passenger, I'd learn about their real estate secrets. And if an entrepreneur got in, I'd dive into how they run their successful business. This way, I turned my cab into a classroom on wheels, learning something new every day. This is how I learnt some of the index fund strategies I explain in chapter 9.

Chapter 6

Driving Smart: Key Mistakes Every Taxi Driver Should Avoid

Remember, being a successful Uber or taxi driver is about more than just driving. It's about providing great service, being efficient, and managing your business wisely.Here are some common mistakes taxi drivers make daily. If you're a taxi driver, you'll want to try and avoid these pitfalls.

1. As mentioned before, one mistake many Uber drivers make is letting riders into their car without verifying their name. When you arrive, especially in a crowded area, you want to ensure you have the right rider. Roll down your window and ask for their name to avoid giving a ride to the wrong person.

2. Do not pick up unaccompanied minors. Many drivers pick up unaccompanied minors, which is a big no-no. If you get a ride request from an elementary school, for example, and find a six-year-old waiting, don't accept the ride. You can't pick up children under 18 unaccompanied, or you risk losing your taxi licence.

3. Do not pick up babies and toddlers without car seats or booster seats. If a rider has a child, they must provide a booster or car seat. Letting a passenger hold their baby is illegal, unsafe, and against policy. If you live in an area where people with toddlers are frequently requesting taxi rides, it is a good idea to keep a small booster seat in your car.

4. Buying a new car for taxi business. Buying a new car for a taxi business means you'll have to pay some of your

earnings to the company that financed the car. You'll also lose money in depreciation expense as the car's value goes down over time, which is explained in Chapter 3.

5. Not driving with a schedule can hinder your earnings. Setting a schedule and sticking to it, like driving airport rides early in the morning, can significantly increase your earnings. Remember you have to treat yourself as a business with fixed opening and closing hours that you respect religiously. Having a schedule is all about efficiency, saving money, building momentum, establishing good habits, and achieving your dreams and goals. Plus, a schedule keeps procrastination at bay.

6. Many drivers try to set an earnings goal daily which means they can get demotivated when they do not meet their daily target. For me I never check how much I have made until at the end of my day.

7. Do not take cash in exchange for rides not booked through rideshare apps. This is illegal and can lead to deactivation.

8. Playing the wrong type of music can negatively impact the rider's experience. Choose neutral, non-offensive music to cater to a broader audience.

9. Driving dangerously or too fast is a no-go. Safe driving ensures a better experience for passengers and reduces the risk of accidents. I see many drivers driving fast at weekends so they can make more money. The irony is they will get tired quickly and go home while the drivers like myself who drive the speed limit and enjoy the ride carry on going.

10. Not driving for both Uber and Lyft and other operators limits your earning potential. Using multiple apps can increase your ride requests and earnings.

11. Eating at restaurants every day costs a lot of money and can use up what you earn. If you spend £15 on food each day, it adds up to £450 in a month. To save money, it's better to bring your own food or eat at home before you go to work.

12. Not cleaning the inside of your vehicle regularly can lead to poor ratings. Keep your car clean to provide a pleasant experience for passengers.

13. Not renewing your documents, like insurance or car inspection, can lead to deactivation in the rideshare apps. Keep your documents up to date because deactivation for a week will cost you at least £1000 in lost earnings.

14. Not greeting passengers by their name can make a poor first impression. A simple greeting can enhance the rider's experience.

15. Not researching your market can mean missing out on lucrative areas or times to drive. Underestimating the value of knowing your city is a common misstep. Get to know the hotspots, the best hotels, restaurants, events, and venues. The more you know, the better your earnings will be.

16. Do not quit your job to drive full-time without first trying it part-time can be risky. Test the waters before making a significant career change. If you have a disability or medical condition that limits you from driving for long hours, it means you are not suited for the taxi business.

17. Driving around looking for rides is inefficient. Stay put and wait for ride requests to save fuel and time.

18. Taking too many passengers than your car can legally hold is illegal and unsafe.

19. Not taking enough breaks and getting enough sleep can lead to burnout and health issues.

20. Not tracking your miles for tax purposes can cost you during tax season.

21 Not going the extra mile for passengers, like helping with luggage, can affect tips and ratings.

22, Renting a car for Uber or Lyft will cost you more in the long run. You can rent for a start but then quickly save money to by a good used car. The peace of mind and flexibility that comes with owing your own car is priceless.

23. You dont have to take every single ride as some rides you take might not be profitable for you.

24 . Not having enough sleep can lead to a whole bunch of issues like depression, clumsiness, a dip in motivation, forgetfulness, and even a weakened immune system. Not to mention, it can mess with your reaction time, which is crucial for avoiding accidents. And falling asleep at the wheel is definitely not part of a successful taxi strategy.

25. Beware of information overload. The internet is swamped with Uber content, but a lot of it is more about entertainment or venting frustrations. If you're spending hours scrolling through forums and social media, you're probably not learning the real tricks of the trade. My advice is to listen to

those who've been in the game for at least two years, have a substantial social media following, and have raked in some serious earnings.

26. Taking too many days off. That's a mistake many new drivers make. Sure, you're self employed and it is your rule, but too much downtime can kill your momentum. Focus on learning the ropes and understanding your own unique business model.

27 .Thinking you know it all. That's a trap. Even with my success, it took me a good eight months to really get the hang of the taxi business. It is good practice to research your market and network with other drivers.

28 Don't let riders overstay their welcome during multi-stop trips. Remember, you only get paid when the wheels are rolling with a passenger inside. Stops should only last 3-5 minutes.

29. During multi-stop trips avoid letting passengers leave their stuff; like purses, phones, or even a child seat in your car. Make it clear they need to take their belongings because you can only wait 3 to 5 minutes.

30. Don't wait forever for a passenger who isn't ready. Once that timer's up, cancel the ride and move on. Time is money, after all.

31. Remember, you can cancel a ride at any time if you feel unsafe. Stay calm, professional, and try to de-escalate any tense situations. And always drop off in a safe, well-lit area.

32. Finally, don't fall into the employee mindset. My golden rule is "If you treat Uber like a job, it will pay you like an employee; and if you treat it like a business, it will pay you like a boss." As a driver, you're the boss, every success and setback falls on you.

Chapter 7

Breaking Free: My Path Out OF DEBT

Both the government and companies want you to spend money. That's how GDP goes up - the more money you spend, the better it is for the economy, and companies profit from it. Each day companies try to find creative ways to make you spend money. They want you hooked to spending money, just like a drug dealer. You get addicted to spending, and they make more money. You buy one thing, then another, and it keeps going. Video games, clothes, you name it. The more you get addicted, the more money they make. And that's fine, it's their business model. But as an individual, you have to make a choice not to fall into this trap because it can be incredibly stressful.

I used to be in debt, £28000 in total. My credit score was very low. Something changes in you when you're in debt. You can't eat well, be a good person. Your temper is short, your patience is thin, and you're irritated with everyone around you because you're in debt, and you don't know how to get out of it. Bankruptcy might seem like an option, but it's incredibly stressful.

60% of the UK's GDP is generated from consumer spending. That is 60% of the GDP comes from people spending money. With interest rates at 5.25% and a high cost of living, consumers are feeling the squeeze. Personal savings rates are at record low. People are not saving much, but they are spending a lot. Politicians may boast about GDP growth, saying it's the best in years. They're right, and it's thanks to you spending money. It's like Saudi Arabia's reliance on oil, 42% of their GDP comes from oil; consumers are like the oil to the UK economy.

Increasingly popular is the Buy Now Pay Later (BNPL) market. This alternative to credit cards, whose popularity surged during the pandemic, is predicted to reach $4 trillion by 2030. Consumers are taking advantage of paying for goods and services in interest-free instalments. Markel Advisers estimate that the number of BNPL users will exceed $1.85 billion by 2030, up from 43 million in the first half of 2023 - that's nearly a 4 times increase in just seven years. Understanding this dynamic sheds light on BNPL – it's another creative way to get money from the consumer, put them into debt as they are usually buying what they do not need. So BNPL is another creative way to extract money from consumers, put them into debt, and ensure they eventually pay. Apple, Barclays bank, Amazon and the other big companies making money from BNPL will always get their money. However, being in debt is far from exciting; it's a burden that affects various aspects of life – parenting, relationships, and more. It's crucial to be aware of the consequences and make wise financial decisions. Some might argue that being in debt is an example of bad capitalism but I dont see it as the case as the responsibility lies with the consumer. Just as a bartender might encourage you to drink, it's your choice to control your decisions. I, too, was once addicted to credit cards and faced a tough financial situation.

Control your decisions, and you can prevent yourself from falling into this temptation.

"He who is quick to borrow is slow to pay." I know this because I've been quick to borrow many, many times. "If you think nobody cares if you're alive, try missing a couple of debt payments." - Earl Wilson. "When you get in debt, you become a slave- Andrew Jackson."

Banks and credit lenders are producing a lot of slaves today. You cannot have financial freedom when you're drowning in debt, and I can tell you that from firsthand experience. You have to realise not all debt is bad, the debt you take out to generate income is a good debt as you will find out in the next chapter.

Back in 2014, I had a council tax debt of £3000 related to a London flat I used to live in since 2010. The debt had been increased to £5000 as charges get added each time the bailiffs call round and I don't pay or I'm not in.

I was relaxing on my bed one saturday morning when I heard a loud knock on my door. Hesitant to open it, the person knocked again, even louder, as if he was about to break down the door. This angered me, as I suspected it might be a delivery person with an excessive amount of energy. I stormed out of the house and was immediately confronted by two bulky bailiffs who had arrived, seemingly prepared for a fight with stab-proof vests and grins on their faces. They told me I had to pay the council tax debt I owed; otherwise, they would take away all my possessions to be auctioned. I called the police, who came and, to my surprise, supported the bailiffs. I had no choice but to arrange a payment plan and pay them all the money in my bank account at the time, which was a measly £400. I further arranged to pay £350 a month going forward until the debt was paid off. However, I then defaulted the following month and went on the run again by moving to a new address. This escape attempt proved short-lived, as they soon discovered my new address when I underwent a credit check while attempting to secure a contract for a new phone. Unfortunately, the credit check failed due to my bad credit, and at the time, I was unaware that credit reference agencies were sharing data with the bailiffs. It didn't take long for the bailiffs to track me down, prompting me to move again to another address.

The council tax debt was just the tip of the iceberg. I owed an additional £18,000 on credit cards, money that I had used to buy designer clothing in an attempt to impress people who, more often than not, didn't even like me. Some of it was also spent on holidays, which I regretted as soon as I returned. With this enormous debt hanging over me, I found myself in a constant state of evasion. I spent several years running away from bailiffs. Ironically, I used to enjoy watching the TV show 'If You Don't Pay, We Will Take It,' where bailiffs go around collecting debts or seizing belongings from people. Then, unexpectedly, I found myself in a situation similar to those depicted in the show.

When I became a taxi driver in 2014, my debt had grown to about £28,000. This was because I had taken an additional £5,000 from my credit card to purchase a car, which I then registered as a taxi. The car in question was a Kia Ceed with an automatic gearbox. Unfortunately, at that time, I hadn't done any research on cars, so I wasn't aware that I should have avoided the Kia model. About 10 months later, the gearbox of the car malfunctioned, and I had no choice but to sell it for spare parts. The fortunate part is that I had managed to pay off all my debts before the car broke down. Fortune favored me on this occasion.

When I began working as a taxi driver, I was lazy and lacked self-motivation. Working more than 30 hours a week was a challenge for me because I would get tired easily. My lack of sleep was partly due to spending excessive time on Netflix and social media, watching silly videos and movies that didn't contribute to my personal development. During this period, my earnings were around £700 a week before expenses, and in London, that doesn't stretch very far. However despite living paycheck to paycheck, I was happy as I was self employed and I did not have a horrible boss. In fact, I enjoyed working as a taxi driver as I found engaging in conversations with people from all walks of life was very entertaining. It was during one of these conversations that the first *eureka moment* occurred when I met Ryan who worked 18 hours a day, as I described in Chapter 4. It was then that I began doing the maths to figure out how I could finally clear my debt and shield myself from the looming threat of bailiffs.

You can read every financial book on how to eliminate debt and watch every debt relief guru on YouTube, but still struggle with debt. Most of them tend to use fancy words without providing concrete guidance on how to generate additional income. Furthermore, they often overlook the fact that hard work is essential. Back when I worked in an office, I was one of those individuals who were overworked but underappreciated. I was determined to prove my strong work ethic.

I use to watch people on YouTube boasting about how they cleared their debts in no time. One woman I watched even claimed she cleared $300,000 of debt in just 15 months, and I couldn't help but wonder how this was possible. One day, in the midst of watching one of these videos, I stopped and said to myself that I was going to be debt-free in six months, especially after gathering inspiration from Ryan - the hardworking old man who had served in the special forces. So I decided it was time to clear my debts. I wrote a note to myself that stated, "I will be totally debt-free by May 15, 2015." I gave myself six months, and I even underlined 'totally.' And guess what? I failed. On May 15, 2015, I was not totally debt-free, but I was on my way.

Another four months later, I finally achieved my goal of being totally debt-free. It took a total of 10 months to clear £28,000 worth of debt.

The initiatives I embraced to eliminate my debts

Remember that if you are not serious about getting out of debt, you will never be debt-free. When I decided to get out of debt, I told myself that I was going to do everything it takes, as long as it's legal and moral, to become debt-free. In 2015, I had had enough, and I wanted to break free from debt. The first thing I did was decide not to take on any new debt, especially avoiding types of debt that had caught me out in the past, such as zero percent financing deals for 12 months. Usually, I would take on something, fully intending to pay it off within 12 months, but then I wouldn't, and the debt would start accruing interest. Also, I decided I will not take out any new credit cards, including balance transfer cards. Many times before, I would transfer a balance to the new card, then end up starting to spend on my old card again, initiating another turbulent cycle.

I also avoided credit cards that claimed to help me rebuild my credit. Despite having bad credit, there were credit card providers eager to offer me a new credit card to assist in rebuilding my credit score. They would send credit card offers via post, and all I had to do was sign and return them. However, all these types of mail went straight to the bin.

This is because I had previously obtained similar credit cards and, unfortunately, ended up spending up to their maximum limits. Consequently, my overall debt increased.

One mistake I was making while having the huge credit card debt was that I was making only the bare minimum repayments on the cards each month. According to my calculations, if I continued this approach, it would have taken me more than 42 years to pay off the £18,000 in credit card debt. And after the 42 years, I would have paid a total of £46,000 to my credit card providers.

I made a rule for myself that whenever I want to buy something, I will use the money I already have in my bank account. I won't use credit cards because I know I wasn't disciplined enough to pay off what I had spent before it started accruing interests. Following this rule helped me to stay on track with my goal of getting out of debt. When I use my debit card or cash, I am using the money I actually have, not borrowing from the future. It prevents me from overspending and accumulating more debt. It's like having a plan for my money – if I have enough in my account, I can buy something; if not, I wait until I can pay for it without using credit.

Using debit cards or cash makes it easier to track my expenses. I can see exactly where my money is going, and it helps me make better financial decisions. With credit cards, it's easy to lose track of how much you've spent, and that can lead to unexpected surprises when the bill arrives. By sticking to debit cards or cash, I have a better grasp of my financial situation, which is crucial for managing and reducing debt effectively. So when it came to buying a phone, I made sure I was buying it outright, not on contract, and I would choose a SIM-only deal with unlimited data. Also, I made sure the network provider caps the maximum amount I can spend in a month. Before my debt troubles, I would get a phone on credit and pay for it bit by bit each month.

Next, I took some radical steps. I cut up my credit cards so I could not spend more, and I made sure I did not save any card numbers to use on the internet. I also deleted all my credit cards saved on my Amazon and eBay accounts, as I used to engage in impulse buying, especially when I came across an advertisement for a product online.

Then I created a spreadsheet on Excel in an attempt to understand where my money was going. On the spreadsheet, I meticulously listed all my debts, noting the owed amount, interest rate, and minimum monthly payments. I also listed who I owed, the balance I owed along with the interest rate, and how much I would have to pay today if I were to pay the debt in full. Additionally, I listed how much I absolutely have to pay each and every month just to meet the minimum payment. For many years, money was being taken out of my account without me knowing what was going on. At this point, I needed to find out every penny I could save to put towards my debt. It became apparent that I had been making many small expenditures that built up to a significant amount. For example, I used to buy McDonald's meals every day for £5.99, which alone added up to about £180 a month. I decided to start making my own meals and invested in a coffee machine to avoid buying coffee when I am out driving. Additionally, I used to spend £20 every week on haircuts, totaling more than £1000 a year. So, I purchased a professional clipper for £60 and learned to cut my own hair. Even though I always gave myself the same simple haircut, it still looked neat and well-done.

Another step I took to clear my debts was deciding to sell all the items I could and put the money towards my debt. I sold my PlayStation along with all the games, which totaled more than 50. I sold my designer clothes for less than a third of what I paid for them. I also sold my Canon DSLR camera, my old laptop, some jewelry, and one of my Bose speakers (I do not know how or why I needed a second set of Bose speakers). The amount raised from the sale of my items was about £1600. Each time I sold an item, even if it was for £5, I would immediately pay the money into one of my credit card accounts, as I had four of them. I became addicted to paying money into my credit card account as I always got excited each time I saw my debt balance reduce.

Then, I called my credit card providers and tried to negotiate a lower interest rate, but they all refused to provide a lower interest rate, even when I told them I was struggling with a lot of debt at the time. I could not even get a good rate on a zero percent balance transfer credit card, as I had a very low credit score. Additionally, I tried to avoid getting a new balance transfer credit card, as I could easily be tempted to start spending on the old card as soon as I transferred the balance to a new card.

Also I decided to significantly reduce my spending. It was really tough, but I didn't have a choice. I decided to stop eating out or going to clubs with my friends. I used to go out with them about once a month, usually on the weekend, because they had regular 9-to-5 jobs. But for me, as a taxi driver, going out on the weekend meant I'd lose a lot of money. In money terms, it's usually about £500 to £1000 that I would miss out on because the day after going out, I'm usually not feeling well, and I can't work. Over a year, this could add up to a huge £12000.

As a way to spend less money, I stopped getting new clothes. I used to buy new clothes from fancy designer stores, and I often went to TKMaxx, buying lots of things I didn't really need. So, I made a decision that going forward, I would only get my clothes from second-hand places like car boot sales and eBay. It was surprising to find designer clothes at car boot sales, but this time, they didn't cost as much. I also stopped buying gadgets. Before, I used to get a new PS4 game every month, but since I had sold my PlayStation console, I could not buy any new titles. Additionally, I realised I'd visited Turkey and Spain enough times, so I made a decision not to spend £1500 every year on holidays to those places. Making these changes helped me save more money.

Looking back, I realise I used to do some silly things. When I was heavier, I'd wear expensive £200 t-shirts and go to bars or nightclubs. Surprisingly, most people there didn't even know it was a designer shirt. And, honestly, I can't recall any girl ever giving me her number just because I was wearing something fancy. But things took a turn when I started the slow carb diet. In just 24 months, I managed to reach a healthy BMI, and that's when my story started to change.

I used to pay for some subscriptions that I didn't really need, so I decided to review my monthly bills to see what I could cut. First, I said goodbye to my gym membership, which was costing me £25 every month, saving me £300 a year. Although I had a gym membership, I barely went there, maybe once or twice a month. Instead, I bought a used under-desk treadmill for £70 and some dumbbells from Facebook Marketplace because I planned to work out in my room. This way, I could stay fit without spending so much on a gym membership. I also ditched my Netflix subscription and sold my TV since that's all I ever watched on it. From then on, I opted to use my laptop for watching movies. I canceled subscriptions to Sky Sports, Amazon prime and Now TV, the only one I kept was YouTube Premium because I needed it for listening to podcasts, music, and documentaries while driving. Moreover, I made sure to secure the cheapest car insurance for my second year as a taxi driver. In the second year, my insurance cost dropped from £3000 to £1500 because I diligently searched and negotiated for hours, highlighting my 8-year no claims discount.

After cancelling all the subscriptions that I didn't need I then diligently checked my bank statements for a few months, examining where my money was going. I went through each item, asking myself two important questions. First, I questioned if I truly needed something I regularly bought. Then, I pondered the "what if" scenario. What if I got rid of these things? How much would it genuinely impact my life? At this point, I made sure that every single penny I saved went straight into my debt account.

The crucial lesson I learned here was that even adding relatively small amounts of money to what I was paying off on my debts each week had a significant impact. It not only decreased the time it took me to get out of debt but also lowered the amount of interest I had to pay. It showed me that every little bit saved could make a big difference in the long run.

At this point I knew I had to increase my income and luckily for me few days back I had been inspired by Ryan , who shared that he used to work 18-hour days. So, I made a decision that when I went out to work, I wouldn't come home until I had earned at least £150 a day from taxi fares, Monday to Thursday. For the weekends, I set a goal to make at least £200 a day from Friday to Sunday. This strategy turned out to be successful, helping me earn an average of £1200 a week. However, it also meant that I had to be out during non-peak hours in order to achieve these goals. This strategy was successful but not smart because I spent longer waiting for rides, often in the cold during winter months. I would later change this strategy and create a better 14 hours work day schedule as I described in chapter 4.

One good thing about being a taxi driver is you can decide to promote yourself and give yourself a raise any day you want by working harder. With my new schedule, which meant I was making about £1800 a week in London, I began putting between £700 to £900 into my debt account every week. I stayed disciplined and focused and 10 months later I had cleared all £28000 worth of debt.

I learnt from watching youtube videos that there are two approaches to paying off debt . The debt avalanche and debt snowball methods. With the debt avalanche method, you focus on paying off your debts with the highest interest rates first. With the debt snowball method, you focus on paying off your smallest debts first, regardless of their interest rates. What I did was clear the balance on my smallest credit card, which was £2500. After that, I called the card provider and asked for a lower interest rate on a balance transfer. Once they agreed, I transferred a smaller balance from the bigger credit card account with a higher interest rate to the one I just cleared. I repeated this process several times until all my debts were paid off in 10 months. So, in a way, I sort of mixed both the debt avalanche and debt snowball methods to tackle my debts

The theory behind the debt snowball method is if you can get out of a debt quickly, psychologically, that's uplifting. That really helps motivate you to keep going on your debt journey, and I think there's some truth behind that, and a lot of studies support that. For me my personal approach was getting wired to the debt just like the programmers in the movie *the social network* got wired to their screens when seriously coding for Facebook. Being wired to my debt meant I was always thinking about it and figuring out ways to clear it every second of the day. This led me to the strategy where I combined elements from both the debt avalanche and snowball methods. Achieving freedom from debt is an incredible feeling. Always remember that the most valuable thing money can provide is financial freedom, which ultimately translates to peace of mind.

Chapter 8

From first property to fortune:
How real estate investing changed my life

Most people will never buy a property and change their lives just because of lack of knowledge. I used to browse real estate listings I could not afford on property websites in the same way 50 Cents gazed at sneakers he couldn't afford through shop windows in the film "Get Rich or Die Tryin'." Most people think too much money is required or they are broke so they cannot buy a property but the reality is they lack the knowledge of property investing just like me a few years ago. In the past 7 years I have bought 14 properties simply because I understand a very specific and niche property strategy which I will explain in this chapter. In the last 3 months one of my friends has bought 6 apartments not because he is a millionaire it is because he has the knowledge on how to go about it.

For most people it is easy to assume that building a property portfolio requires a substantial amount of money but they are creative ways of acquiring properties that will change your life. You might need to work a bit hard to save up and start up but when you get going the sky's the limit. The best thing to do is to understand all the property investing strategies then pick which one works for you based on your specific goals and circumstances and how much time you have available. Don't waste your time paying attention to those negative stories on the internet that make property investing seem impossible.

I got into property investing by chance, as a series of experiences I call 'eureka moments' led me to this point in my life. One such moment was when I met an Uber driver while visiting Manchester, and he told me he owns seven houses. I was amazed at how he got seven houses, but I wasn't looking to buy many houses at the time. I just wanted one affordable place to live. In the quest to own a single property, I discovered a way to acquire multiple properties that I now use to generate income. There are various property investing strategies, but before jumping into the bandwagon, I explored the popular strategies circulating, especially on the internet, along with their pros and cons.

When looking to choose the right property investing strategy for you, it's all about understanding what your plans and goals are long-term. Quite simply, there are two ways to invest in a property: the first is to buy a property and then hold it with the idea of renting it out to a tenant; the second is buying a property and flipping it, or refurbishing it, with the idea of selling it. Under the 2 main strategies there are five sub strategies that you can consider today that balance time, money, and experience. The main thing here is considering whether your strategy or your plan is all about cash flow, or whether it's about capital appreciation and growth of your initial seed money that you have.

The strategies I explored before I got started were: buy-to-lets, HMOs, serviced accommodation, flipping properties, investing in commercial property, and the internet's favourite BRRRR strategy.

Buy-to-let

The first main strategy is simple vanilla buy-to-let. This is when you purchase a property to rent it out and make money from the rent payments. Most beginner property investors do start with this particular strategy. It's very easy, low risk, requires less capital upfront to purchase a house, and it's a very easy method. All you need to do is have enough money for a deposit. This will enable you to buy a property that you can rent out.

Buy-to-let mortgages has the most availability with good interest rates. With Buy-to-let you want to make sure you know how to evaluate a property deal, and if you get your numbers right, then you can make a really decent three to five hundred pounds a month profit after all of the costs, if you choose the right house and the right area. Here's an example breakdown of the figures for a typical 2 bedroom buy-to-let property investment.

Purchase Price	£80,000
Deposit (25%)	£20,000
Stamp Duty (3%)	£2,400
Legal Fees	£1,000
Mortgage Amount (75%)	£60,000
Monthly Mortgage Repayment	£175
Rental Income	£500
Gross Income	£325

Notice that If you work hard as an Uber driver and save £1,000 each week, you can gather the £20,000 needed for a deposit in 20 weeks or 5 months. This means you could own 10 properties of this kind in 5 years. When I spoke to the Uber driver who owned 7 houses, I didn't understand it then.

Here are some of the pros and cons of buy-to-let property investing:

It's great for beginners and there are often loads of different mortgage products available on the market, so therefore they're competitive. People who rent and live in these homes tend to stay for a long time. This is often because they are families who prefer not to change homes frequently. There's little effort once the tenant has moved in, especially if you're using a managing agent. It's very easy to calculate your sums to work out profit, return on investment, and yield. And lastly, because house prices especially up north in the UK are typically cheaper, it means that you need a low deposit to get started.

One downside of buy-to-let is that, when you factor in all the costs and everything involved in buying and renting the property, it doesn't generate as much money at the end of the month compared to other strategies that bring in more cash flow.

Another disadvantage of buy-to-let is legislation. You need to make sure that you stay in line with new legislation and understand all the different documentation and certificates that you're required to present and show to your tenant upon moving into your property. Another downside is that if your investment property is located far from where you are, you usually need to pay a managing agent, and this fee is typically around 10% to 15%.

House in Multiple occupation (HMO)

The second major property investing strategy is Houses of Multiple Occupancy, otherwise known as an HMO property. This is usually for students or young professionals who share a house with lots of different people and you all have your own different contract. Usually there will be a shared kitchen and bathroom in the house. It works really well for students and for young working professionals who might just need to be in a city for 12 to 18 months, for example. The whole idea of an HMO property is rather than renting out the entire house for a fixed fee, you instead rent out each individual room. Having a house with several bedrooms can often generate more income as an HMO compared to what you would earn through buy-to-let on the same property. For example, if you purchase a 2-bedroom house for £80,000 and convert it into a 3-bedroom HMO by transforming the living room into an additional bedroom, the rental income will increase from £500 to £900, as shown in the following table.

Purchase Price	£80,000
Deposit (25%)	£20,000
Stamp Duty (3%)	£2,400
Legal Fees	£1,000
Mortgage Amount (75%)	£60,000
Monthly Mortgage Repayment	£175
Rental Income	£900
Gross Income	£725

There are many laws and regulations governing HMOs. If you're interested in getting into HMOs, the best step is to search for your local council along with the term 'HMO' on Google. This is so you can find the specific requirements from your local council, including details about room sizes, kitchen dimensions, the number of hobs and cookers required per a certain number of people, and any necessary fire safety measures.

One advantage of HMOs is that you don't necessarily have to purchase a large five-bedroom house. You could consider two or three-bedroom houses, and all you have to do is transform the living room into a bedroom. If there's an attic room, you can also add an extra bedroom there. This is how you can convert a two or three-bedroom property into a five or six-bedroom property.

The last thing you should consider with an HMO property is there are lots of popular developing areas where HMOs exist. And because there are so many HMOs in these areas, councils are introducing something called Article 4. Article 4 isn't something new, it has been around for a while. Under an Article 4 direction, landlords may need to seek planning permission to convert a dwelling into an HMO, which they would not have needed to do under the general permitted development rights. This is often used in areas where there is a desire to maintain the character of a community or to manage the number of HMOs in a particular area, due to concerns about over-concentration of rental properties and its potential impacts on local communities. It's important to check the specific regulations in your local area or consult a legal professional for advice regarding HMO regulations and the implications of Article 4 directions.

HMO properties have several advantages. Firstly, they tend to generate more cash flow compared to traditional buy-to-let properties. Secondly, even if one tenant leaves a room in an HMO, the property continues to generate income from the other rented rooms. Lastly, experienced landlords can benefit by converting buy-to-let properties into HMOs, especially when a family moves out. This conversion allows landlords to maximize the property's potential, squeezing more value and increasing the overall earning capacity.

One disadvantage of an HMO property is that it requires a lot of knowledge on HMO legislation. They're typically a little bit more expensive to get up and run, especially if you plan on decorating the place really well. Good mortgage rates are quite difficult to come across for HMOs if you don't have prior buy-to-let experience. And typically, tenants tend to stay for between 12 and 18 months in terms of their tenancies, meaning you might have one or more months without tenants.

Serviced accommodations

The next property investing strategy is serviced accommodations, my preferred approach. This is usually an apartment where you stay for a short time just like a hotel but unlike a hotel the apartment has all the amenities of a family home like a kitchen with a fridge-freezer and a washing machine. Serviced accommodations are commonly booked via platforms like Airbnb or booking.com. With the growth of Airbnb over the past few years, there has been an explosion of serviced accommodation properties. At the moment, because this is quite new and the government is quite slow to keep up with different trends, so there's not a huge amount of legislation around serviced accommodations.

A decent flat in a city centre that has all the right permissions to be a serviced accommodation can generate a good few thousand pounds a month if the occupancy rate is high enough. But one thing to bear in mind is seasonal impacts. If you have a holiday cottage in Cornwall, then one thing to remember is that you'll have a higher cash flow in the summer months, but as you get towards winter and things slow down, you're going to have more void periods. Therefore, your occupancy rate is going to go down, and the property won't earn as much as it potentially could do.

While profits can be good with serviced accommodations, it requires a lot of effort. You have to set up automated systems to handle cleaners, laundry, and changing the bedding to ensure the place is clean every time guests leave. Because there are many different parts and systems involved, there's more chance for things to go wrong. If your property is far away, like five hours, it could become a big problem for you.

Even though there are challenges and it involves a lot of work, let's say you have a serviced apartment in Manchester that rents out for £95 per night. If you manage to rent it out for 20 days in a month, that would give you a total of £1,900 in rental income for that month. Here's a breakdown of the numbers for a typical serviced accommodation property.

Purchase Price	£80,000
Deposit (25%)	£20,000
Stamp Duty (3%)	£2,400
Legal Fees	£1,000
Mortgage amount (75%)	£60,000
Monthly Mortgage repayment	£175
Rental Income	£1900
Gross Rental Income	£1725

Flipping houses

The fourth property investing strategy is flipping houses. This is really popular in the UK, and we have many programs on TV, one of them is "Homes Under the Hammer," where you see people go to an auction, buy a property for a really cheap price, spend ten or twenty thousand pounds on a refurb, and then resell the house for a profit. It's probably not profitable every single time in reality, but if you understand the figures and the cost of a refurb on the property that you're buying, then it can be very lucrative. You can make a good lump sum of about 10 to 30 thousand pounds, depending on the price of the property that you're buying and how much money you're putting into the refurb.

The big risk in flipping a property is if you make mistakes with your calculations or don't really know the house prices in a specific area. In this case, you might end up investing a lot of your money in just one deal. There's also a chance you buy a property and find out that the renovation costs more than what you have. This leaves you with a project you can't finish because you don't have enough money to complete it. As a result, you can't sell it and make a profit, and in the end, you might end up losing money.

The best way to make a profit when flipping a property is to buy that particular property below market value for comparables in the area. You can't just go to a nice family home and ask for a 20% discount; they're just not going to sell it to you like that, and no estate agent is going to accept this kind of offer. However if you find a property that's unloved or has a particular problem with it, for example, Japanese knotweed, structural problems, an expiring lease, or something fixable, you can use these issues to negotiate a lower price. Once you've purchased the property and addressed the issue, its value will go up, allowing you to sell it and make a profit.

One key here is to understand the difference between asking price and market value. You might see a property on *Rightmove* or *Zoopla* that is selling for £120,000. You might also see that comparables of the exact same size of house and bedrooms in the area are only selling for £100,000. This doesn't mean that the property you're looking at is worth £120,000. It means the asking price is £120000, but the true market value might only be £100,000. So, if you offer £100,000, you're not getting it below market value; you're getting it at market value, and that's something to consider. Some new property investors do make this mistake when valuing a property.

Property flipping can be lucrative as you can make £30,000-£40,000 profit on one really good deal, which is more than the average salary in the UK. But in terms of a mortgage and lending perspective, you need to show lenders that you have experience of managing a build team and managing a refurbishment project before you can truly unlock things like development finance. Also, to make the most profit, you have to improve the property, like adding an additional bedroom, bathroom, or kitchen. Last year, my friend bought a house with 2 bedrooms for £140,000. He spent £21,000 to fix it up and added another bedroom, making it a 3-bedroom house. Then, he sold the house for £190,000. He made a profit of £29,000.

Commercial property

Lastly, but not least, property investing strategy is investing in commercial property. This is a strategy that hasn't truly been explored yet by a lot of property investors. It is nowhere near as popular in the commercial market as it is in the residential market. The great thing with commercial property is that because there is less competition, it means that there are more opportunities available.

A commercial property strategy could be as simple as buying a shop local to you that has a flat upstairs and a shop on the ground floor. And this means that you can split the property so you can have a small cafe or shop on the ground floor, and then have tenants living above paying rent. In this scenario, there are two separate sources of income. An advantage here is, if there's a family living in the apartment above, they are likely to stay for a long period. Additionally, commercial leases usually extend from 5 to 25 years, making commercial tenants truly long-term occupants.

One key thing in the commercial world is the type of lease that you'll have. If you have a buy-to-let property and something breaks within it, it's your responsibility as the landlord to fix it. But within the commercial world, they have what are called FRI leases, which is a Fully Repairing and Insuring lease. Therefore, the tenant who moves in has to insure it, make any repairs as required. Therefore, you as the landlord is very hands-off.

A drawback of investing in commercial property is that it's heavily influenced by the economy. When the COVID lockdown happened, there was a significant move towards online shopping. While there may have been a recovery to some extent, the dynamics of the traditional shopping areas are constantly evolving. If you're considering entering the commercial property market, it's crucial to have various exit strategies and a contingency plan. For instance, if retail stores become less popular, you should think about alternative uses for the space on the high street in the future.

The BRRRR Strategy

BRRRR is an acronym, coined by Brandon Turner of BiggerPockets, representing five key steps for smartly investing in a rental property. BRRRR is an abbreviation for Buy, Repair (or Rehab or Renovate), Rent, Refinance, and Repeat.

How BRRRR Works

Buy: You buy a rental property below it's market value. This typically involves a property that needs some repairs.

Repair: You then repair, rehab, or renovate the property so you can attract tenants who will pay the monthly rent to live in the property.

Rent: Once the property is rented to good tenants, the property starts generating income, thereby increasing the property's value.

Refinance: Once you can show a lender that you are making money from this property and that you have equity in it, you should be able to do a cash-out refinance.

Repeat: Buy another property and do it all over again.

THE BRRRR METHOD

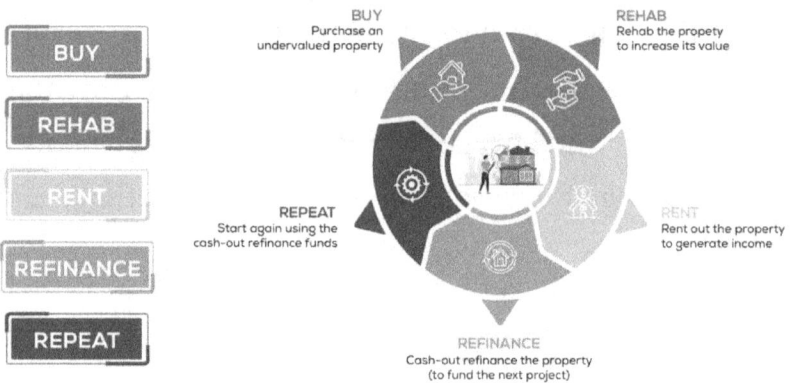

BUY
REHAB
RENT
REFINANCE
REPEAT

BUY
Purchase an
undervalued property

REHAB
Rehab the propety
to increase its value

REPEAT
Start again using the
cash-out refinance funds

RENT
Rent out the property
to generate income

REFINANCE
Cash-out refinance the property
(to fund the next project)

The BRRRR strategy works best with properties you can get for below market value or in other words, homes that aren't move-in-ready. Here's an example that explains why. Let's say you've found a house listed for £120,000 in "as-is" condition. Based on the comparable homes in the area, you determine that this home should be worth £150,000, assuming it's improved and in good shape. Let's also say this home has been on the market for a while and has had at least one price reduction. If you're a good negotiator or you're working with a decent real estate agent, your offer should be less than the asking price for this home.

Suppose you end up buying the house for £110,000. This means you put down a deposit of 25%, which is £27,500 and get a loan for £82,500 to cover the full purchase price. You invest an additional £15,000 in improvements to make it ready for renting. You'll also have a couple more expenses to factor in: stamp duty at 3% that is £3300 and £1000 for legal fees. So £4,300 in total. Then the mortgage payments (£247 times 2) and utilities (£150 times 2) while the house is under renovation (we could assume a vacancy period of two months in this example).

Let's recap the numbers so far.

List Price	£120,000
Sales Price	£110,000
Down Payment	£27,500
Loan Amount	£82,500
Stamp Duty	£3,300
Mortgage Repayment	£494
Utilities	£300
Renovation cost	£15,000
Potential After Repair Value (ARV)	£150,000

The Refinance Part of BRRRR

Okay, so you bought the home, made the repairs, and now you're collecting rent. Since you've made some big improvements, the home is now appraised at a whopping £150,000. Congrats!

Now that the overall value has jumped from £110,000 to £150,000 (with verifiable income from the tenants who are now paying rent), you can essentially hit the 'reset' button by refinancing the loan, because the bank will now look at your property with a new set of eyes, with an appraised value of £150,000. Most conventional banks will typically refinance up to 75% of an investment property's appraised value – so in this case, you'd be able to squeeze £112,500 out of the property's £150,000 value. With this new £112,500 loan amount – you'll be able to pay off your original £82,500 bank loan and have an extra £30,000 leftover... and guess what? That's enough for you to buy another rental property and start the process all over again!

Once you've been through your first BRRRR project, there's virtually no limit to how many more properties you can repeat the process with, because after your first deal is done, you'll be using the bank's money for every future project. Of course realistically you'll probably encounter obstacles that make this process difficult to continue forever (changing interest rates, fluctuating markets, risk-averse banks, etc), but even so, there is beauty in the concept... however long you can run with it.

The fact that your original property (which grew substantially in value) will continue to generate enough income to pay for itself and put money in your pocket each month. And you can use the refinanced value from that first property to continue buying and improving more cash flowing investment properties, all without tying up much (or any) of your own money. It's pretty cool!

Every investor is completely different with different risk appetites. My advice to you is to do your homework on every single strategy. Think about whether you want cash flow in the future or whether you want to build up your capital first. Maybe you want to think about how much time you have available and what your current expertise is today. Every strategy has different pros and cons, and it really is just weighing up the difference between all of them and what you feel resonates best with you to help you achieve your goals in the future.

Overall, there's no right or wrong answer when it comes to property investing. If you are courageous like me you can jump in but if you are not courageous I recommend you speak to a qualified professional, whether that's your accountant, a solicitor, or a broker, and really understand what is best for your own individual situation because they are the only people who can give you accredited advice.

My personal journey into property investing

My journey into property was all by chance. Firstly I had as passenger in my car an old man who told me he had bought his house in 1971 for £7000 and at the time he was earning £5000 per year. This was a eureka moment that made me understand that house prices are inflated especially in London. So I went on property websites like *RightMove* and *Zoopla* to find cheap houses around the UK. What I wanted was a cheap house that I could buy for cash because at the time even though I had paid off my debts I had to rebuild my credit score for a few months before I could be eligible for a mortgage.

I discovered that up in Liverpool some auction properties were listed with guide prices of around £20,000, and that got me excited. I began following live auctions online and realised that these type of properties with a guide price of around £20,000 usually sold for anywhere between £40,000 and £60,000. I was thrilled when I found this out, so I decided to visit Liverpool on an auction date and witnessed experienced landlords swiftly acquiring the auction properties. At the time, all I really needed was just one property.

After the auction was over, I had conversations with several landlords and was astonished by the number of houses some of them possessed. There was one landlord with around 200 houses across the UK. It made me wonder why schools didn't teach us important things like personal finance, how to take out a mortgage, or even how to buy a house at auction. In my opinion, there should be a GCSE subject on property investing because purchasing a house is one of the most significant decisions people will have to make in their lives.

While in Liverpool, I decided to casually chat with taxi drivers to get an idea of how much they could potentially earn. That's when I met an Uber driver from Libya who told me that he was making £1400 a week, working 65 hours. That revelation convinced me to move to Liverpool as the people were friendly, houses were affordable, and I could still make over £1000 as a taxi driver.

After relocating to Liverpool, I was making on average £1550 each week by working for both a local taxi firm and Uber. Although it was less than the £1800 I earned in London, my living costs were lower with rent of only £475 for a two-bedroom flat. Later on, I decided to rent out one of the rooms in the flat for £300 a month since I was usually away working most of the time.

After doing some calculations, I realised I needed about £50,000 to buy a house at auction. So, I made up my mind to save up £50,000 within the next 12 months. At the time, my weekly take-home pay, after covering expenses and food, was hovering at around the £1,000 mark. I believed saving £50,000 in a year was doable because back when I was 11 years old in 1992, I set my sights on a GameBoy handheld game console. It took me two years to save up £60 to finally get it so I was aware that I possessed the talent for saving money somewhere within me. I vividly recall breaking open my piggy bank at the store that sold the GameBoy. The owner and I counted the money together. We realised we were 1p short, and I couldn't hold back my tears. However, the kind shop owner felt sorry for me and gave me the game console. That same saving mentality from my childhood was what I intended to adopt to save £50,000 within a year. I even wrote a note to myself stating, 'By June 30th, 2016, I would have £50,000 or more in my Lloyds Bank savings account.'

Once I began working to save up the £50,000, my VW Passat's diesel particulate filter (dpf) decided to give me trouble. This experience is why I wouldn't recommend using a modern-day diesel car for a taxi business. After unsuccessful attempts to replace the filter, I made the decision to sell the car and opted for a Skoda Rapid with a petrol engine. The Skoda turned out to be reliable, and its parts were affordable.

By June 30th, 2016, I had saved £38,000 instead of the targeted £50,000. Undeterred, I continued working 14-hour days, seven days a week. Finally, in November 2016, I achieved my savings goal of £50,000, and that's when I headed to the auction. I ended up purchasing a 2-bedroom house for £48,000. I couldn't believe I could snap up a house at such a reasonable price just one mile from Liverpool city centre. Despite having only two bedrooms, the house had two living rooms, sparking the idea of converting it into a 4-bedroom serviced accommodation. To handle the legal aspects, I went with my local high street solicitor to complete the deal. I strongly recommend never using a solicitor or conveyance company that you can't physically walk into and have a conversation with, even if they come recommended by the auction house or estate agent.

When dealing with auction properties, there are risks to consider. One approach I took to minimise risks was to focus on terrace houses with two neighbours on each side. This way, I could be more certain about the absence of significant structural issues. Then always, I would have a chat with the neighbours to confirm that the drainage was in good working order. Additionally, I made sure to check the house for any problems like large cracks on the walls or the presence of Japanese Knotweed.

I was really excited that I had bought a house finally even though the house I had purchased was in a pretty bad shape, but then it had taken me just under two years of working as a taxi driver to clear all my debts and to buy the house outright without a mortgage. This would never have been possible with my office job. I felt like a superhero. However, when I started reaching out to tradesmen for refurbishment quotes, I realised there was a massive shortage of skilled workers like plumbers, electricians, plasterers, joiners, and tilers. It seemed like everyone has been pushed to go to university, leaving a shortage of people entering the trades. Most of the tradesmen I contacted quoted me prices that seemed unreasonably high. Based on these quotes, I initially thought I needed around £20,000 to complete the refurbishment. Surprisingly, I managed to get the job done with only £5,000. Now, how did I pull that off?

One day, after receiving another quote from a tradesman that didn't sit well with me, I thought, why not do the work by myself? At that time I had watched countless episodes of 'Homes under the hammer' where I saw people do their own refurb. So I decided to invest in some training. I enrolled in a six-week program at YTA Training in Bradford, covering plumbing, joinery, tiling, kitchen fitting, and plastering. The total cost was around £2000, and it turned out to be one of the best investments I've made. Since completing the training, I've gained a significant advantage in the property development field, saving over £200,000 that I would have otherwise spent on tradesmen over the past seven years. I've read many books suggesting investments in training and self-development, but it never occurred to me that this training could also include DIY courses.

Armed with the new knowledge I had acquired from YTA, I absolutely transformed my house from an old grotty piece of mess to a brand new looking house. I put in a new toilet and kitchen with laminate flooring. I also re-plastered and painted the whole house. The plastering was the part I wish I did not do as it was too labour intensive and cost me a lot in time I could have otherwise been earning money as a taxi driver. I converted the house into a 4 bedroom HMO and listed it on Airbnb and booking.com and immediately started earning money.

The refurb cost me just £5000 as I saved cost by buying a used kitchen from facebook market place and resprayed the cabinets at a cost of £300 then I installed a new worktop. The house had 2 chimney breasts which I knocked down as they were running through both living rooms and bedrooms. This created a lot of extra space. As the chimney breasts were wider than 135mm I had to support the remaining chimney in the loft with a small steel beam as required by legislation. To do this I had to pay a labourer to work with me. I have never learnt how to remove a chimney breast but just from watching YouTube videos and from the confidence I had developed from completing the DIY courses I completed the task with ease.

When the refurb was all done as I was moving from my rented flat into my own house, the owner of the estate agency which managed my rented flat came to check that I had not damaged anything. As he filled out the paperwork for me to sign, I asked him how he became an estate agent. He told me 10 years back he was a truck driver but then he started buying properties for buy-to-let and now owns 15 houses and manages 40 houses for other people. Then another eureka moment happened when he told me I could now borrow against my house and buy another property then do it up then repeat the process just like he has done. So I went back and started researching the BRRRR method.

After watching countless of videos about the BRRRR method I contacted a mortgage broker then I had someone come and valued my house at £70,000. At that time, even though my credit score wasn't very good, I managed to secure a cash-out refinancing for my home. This meant I took on a new 25-year mortgage with an interest rate of 5%, which allowed me to receive £40,000. Consequently, my monthly mortgage payments became £233, and the £40,000 was deposited as cash into my bank account. With the £40000 I added £10000 of my own savings and went back to auction to get a different house. I never borrow more than £40,000. And as I was buying with cash from an auction and not via a mortgage deal which takes longer I am able to complete the process of buying a house and repeat quicker. The only thing that slows me down is the time it takes to refurbish the house.

Buying a house at auction is like going to the super market and buying a can of beans. So far since 2016 I have bought 14 houses, 3 of them bought outright with my own cash and 11 from cash got through refinance deals as explained above. As explained, my approach resembles the BRRRR method, but with a twist—I buy properties through auctions and lease them as serviced accommodations.

MY BRRRR METHOD

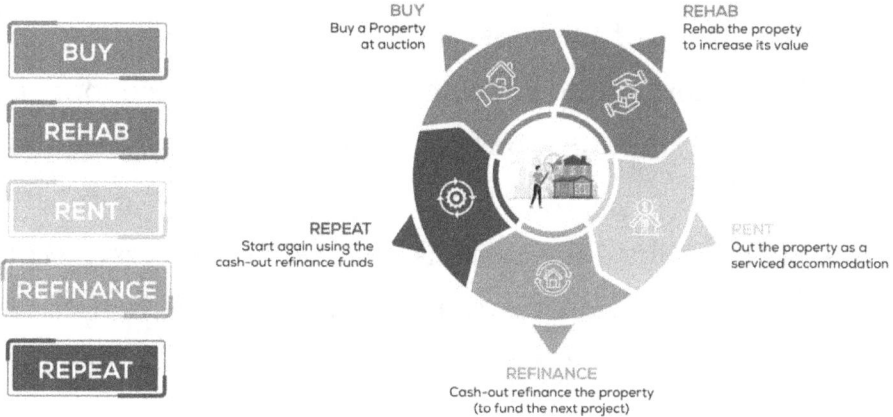

BUY
Buy a Property
at auction

REHAB
Rehab the propety
to increase its value

REPEAT
Start again using the
cash-out refinance funds

RENT
Out the property as a
serviced accommodation

REFINANCE
Cash-out refinance the property
(to fund the next project)

BUY

REHAB

RENT

REFINANCE

REPEAT

Notice that if you have enough money ready, you can buy unlimited houses in just one day at an auction. Unlike traditional ways of buying houses, auctions are fast. Having cash helps because you don't need to wait for loans or other financial stuff. This is good for people who want to quickly get several different properties or take advantage of a good market. But, it's important to be careful and check everything about the houses before buying them to make sure it's a smart investment.

Since I began attending auctions, I've connected with landlords looking to rent out some of their properties. This has allowed me to acquire an additional 5 houses that I don't own. The arrangement involves me paying £400 per month for each property, and in return, I can rent them out as serviced accommodations. Additionally, I'm responsible for the repairs and maintenance of these properties for the next 10 years based on our agreement. Altogether, I now manage a total of 19 properties.

All the houses I own and manage are rented out as serviced accommodations on platforms like Airbnb and booking.com. My approach on these platforms is to compete based on pricing. I like to think of myself as the "easyJet" of serviced accommodations. I typically list my houses at around £1 or £2 less than the average or sometimes the cheapest options in the area. Since all my furniture and appliances are new (purchased from ibidder.com auctions), I'm currently maintaining an average occupancy of 20 days across all the houses, and I've accumulated numerous positive reviews from clients, and a majority of them are repeat customers.

In total all my 19 houses generate a net revenue of £22,000 on an average month, to just above £30,000 in a busy month. As at 2023 prices all my 14 houses are now valued at a minimum of £85,000 each making the networth of my portfolio at least 1.2 million pounds.

As all my properties were bought at auction it means at the end of the mortgage terms I will own all the houses. With buy-to-let mortgages if they are interest only, you do not own the house at the end of the mortgage term. At the time of writing I am in the process of buying a fourth house outright. I am also currently negotiating to refinance the 3 houses that I own outright. As explained I can keep acquiring multiple houses all from one house. I have gone from £28000 in debt to a portfolio worth just over one million pounds in under 8 years. If I can come from a council estate and I am able to do this then I believe any other person can do it. Notice that by applying the money-saving techniques I've learned during my time as a taxi driver, I could have potentially purchased a £200,000 property outright over the eight years of working in this profession if I wanted to.

You never ever want to do a cash out refinance to buy a boat or car as this will just get you back into debt. Lenders like to give out secured loans especially if they realise you are good at investing the money. It is always good to shop around for the best refinance deals. For tax savings only my first house was bought in my name, the rest were bought under my limited company.

My Cashflow from 19 properties

Month to month my properties currently generate anywhere from £22,000 to £30,000 in revenue. I have 14 houses bought for cash at auction and 5 houses I am renting at £400 on a rent to rent strategy from other landlords. Of the 14 houses I own 3 outright and 11 were bought through refinance deals meaning I typically pay about £233 monthly for the mortgages. The below is the income breakdown from my typical month. I have been conservative and used the worst case scenario as £70 per night is the least I will rent a house for on Airbnb or booking.com.

	Number of houses	Total
Rental Income (£70 per day at 20 days occupancy)	19	£26,600
Mortgage payment (14 houses @ £233 each)	14	£3,262
Rent payment (5 houses @ £400 each)	5	£2,000
Gross Income		£21,338

Checks to do before buying an auction property

When considering buying a property at auction, thorough preparation is key to avoid potential pitfalls. Start by reviewing the legal pack with a solicitor to understand any legal obligations and the property's details. A property survey is critical to identify any structural issues or repairs needed, as auction properties often require significant work. Ensure your finances are ready, with a 10% deposit for auction day and the ability to complete the purchase within 28 days. Viewing the property in person is essential to assess its condition and suitability for your needs.

Research the local property market to determine a realistic value and set a maximum bid accordingly. Lastly, plan for unexpected costs by setting aside a contingency fund. These steps will help you make an informed decision and potentially secure a valuable investment at auction.

Finding the best houses for Airbnb

The first step is to locate an area you are familiar with. You want to be investing close to home where you know the area. So, if you're based in Birmingham, start looking at Birmingham to begin with. If you're based in Manchester, look at Manchester. If you're in Edinburgh, look at Edinburgh. Ultimately, if you're in an area where there are lots of people, and there are jobs, and there are things going on, then that's okay. So, start with areas that you're familiar with, that aren't too far from home. Another really important reason for this is, when you get a serviced apartment, it's going to be a bit of work. You'll have to go back and forth to clean, change sheets, furnish, and if it's a three-hour drive, it'll make things really challenging.

The next step is to review the regulations related to serviced accommodations in the specific area where you plan to invest. For instance, in London, there's a 90-day rule. This means you need planning permission if you intend to lease your apartment or house for short-stay lets for more than 90 days in a year. In England, London is currently the only area that has this rule, but there are other legal requirements that you need to look at. For example, if you're buying a property with the intention of renting it out on short-stay lets, you need to make sure that your mortgage lender allows you to do that. If you're doing a rent-to-rent, you need to make sure that your landlord gives you permission to rent it out on Airbnb. So, there are legal requirements that you need to be mindful of before you go ahead. If you're in an apartment block, there might be a head lease restriction that prevents you from renting out a property within the block on short-stay lets. So, look at the legalities and make sure that you have the green light to go ahead.

Another thing to consider before using a property for short term lets is access. Your guests coming to check in are going to need access to the property, and they are going to need access without you being there. If you have to go and let guests in every time, this is just going to be an absolute nightmare. So, you need to put a key safe outside the property. There are some properties or apartment blocks where this isn't convenient, as there may be an awkward gate or maybe the freeholder doesn't allow key safes on the block. So, you need to think, before you take on an apartment. Think about how your guests are going to get in.

When considering purchasing a house for short-term rentals, ensure it is within 5 miles of a major city center. Additionally, choose an area with tourist attractions and amenities such as a football club to attract people to the area. Although you are going to get some business professionals and contractors, generally you will get more bookings from tourists. To find out if there are tourist attractions in an area you can do a Google search about "Things to do in Manchester" for example. If there are concert arenas, museums, theatres, and football clubs then it's a good sign that there's going to be tourists in that area.

Also, before you buy a house, do your due diligence. For example, check the Airbnb listings of others. Observe their booking calendars to gauge how frequently they are reserved and note the rates they are charging. Look at hotels in the area, go on Booking.com, and search for rooms in the area, and if they are frequently booked up, that's a really good sign that your property is going to be booked up as well.

So in summary make sure an area has tourists, then do your due diligence and market research. Next check the legal requirements and access. If all is good then congratulations, you found your perfect rental Airbnb apartment.

Chapter 9

The Route to riches
My Strategy With Index Funds for Yearly Profits

Did you know if you invest £150 per month at nine percent annual return, then in 45 years, you would have over one million pounds? When someone first explained this was possible by investing in index funds, I hardly understood a word they were saying. It was like they were speaking a different language. I wish I knew this when I was younger. Quick disclaimer though, I'm not a financial advisor, this is just a real-life strategy that has worked for me.

I have always considered index funds as a fallback option. Had my property investment strategy not worked out, my plan was to achieve millionaire status through investing in index funds. I'm 43 years old, so why wait 45 years to be a millionaire? I've therefore devised my own investment strategy using index funds that will pay me £100,000 annually starting 15 years from now until the end of my life. I call it my Super Pension. I'll explain the mathematics behind it later.

I have heard all kinds of lies about investing all my life. For instance, at school, when I was growing up, I remember asking my teachers about investing, and they always said it's just for rich people as they can afford to hire professionals to do it for them. For a long time, I believed investing was not for me because I wasn't a professional, and I did not have much money, and I thought I would not stand a chance. Every time I mentioned investing to my family, they seemed so scared because they thought it's the most risky thing in the world and not for normal people. My best friend even said if I started investing, I would lose all my money. Then I had as a passenger in my taxi a hedge fund manager who told me I could not go wrong with index funds, that even banks were investing in index funds.

Professionals and the news make index fund investing look difficult but in fact it is extremely easy to do. You don't need much money to start, the risks are very low, and on average, it will make you more money in the long term compared to other investments. The dark truth is that the average actively managed fund returns two percent less a year compared to the market which index funds track. This means that professionals, on average, are doing worse than index funds, and even if they end up losing your money, they still charge you fees no matter what. According to the movie, "The Matrix," understanding index funds and the power of compounding is like you have taken the red pill and you've woken up to the truth.

When I first started investing in index funds 3 years ago, I felt like I was going to make many mistakes. But once I understood the financial jargon used, it all became so much easier.

So what are index funds and why are they so cool? I'm a big football fan, and if you have ever followed any sports, you'll be familiar with a league table. The better your team performs, the higher up they'll be on the league table. But on the other hand, if they do really badly, they might be removed from the league entirely. This is almost exactly the same as an index fund. All you have to do is switch out the teams for companies. Let's take the S&P 500, for example. This is a list of the 500 best performing public companies in the USA. The big dogs being Amazon, Google,

Apple, and more recently, Tesla. And just like a league table, if a company doesn't perform well, it gets removed from the list.

The concept of an index fund is quite clever; it enables you to invest in every company on the list with a single click. It's a bit like a friend of mine who picks a different football team each year; he just wants to pick the winner every time. So investing in index funds means that even if a few companies do terribly, then it's balanced out by the companies that are doing extremely well.

The average return on the S&P 500 over the last 10 years has been 13.6%. No one has ever lost any money by buying and holding the S&P 500 index fund for more than 20 years. Some people ask if this is so foolproof, then why do people still buy individual stocks? People like to do this because they are speculating to get higher returns which are higher than the market. Some companies might be working on some awesome technology for the future but aren't making a lot of money at the moment, so they won't make the cut into the popular index funds. So now and again, people like to invest into these up-and-coming companies so they don't miss out when the company becomes profitable with the stock value going up. If you had bought $1,000 worth of Tesla shares at its IPO in 2010, with the stock splits adjusted, you would have approximately 882.35 shares at the time of writing this book in 2024. With the current stock price of Tesla at \$184.02, your investment would now be worth approximately \$162,370.59. So if you know how to pick stocks you can get higher returns but it comes with higher risks too.

One man who has had great documented success with stocks is Tim Sykes. He made a lot of money by trading penny stocks, which are low-priced stocks. He started with a small amount of money, but through careful research and smart strategies, he turned it into millions. Tim not only made money but also teaches others how to do it through educational programs. His success story shows that with the right approach, even small investments can lead to big gains in the stock market.

Another famous example of someone who has made money in stocks is Warren Buffett. Warren Buffett became really rich by investing in companies that he thought were undervalued and had strong foundations. He started with a textile company and made smart choices, like investing in Coca-Cola. Instead of quickly buying and selling, he held onto his investments for a long time. This patient and careful strategy, along with smart acquisitions, helped him build a massive wealth over many years. Warren Buffett's success teaches us that being patient and choosing good companies can lead to making lots of money in the stock market.

How to invest tax free

You will often hear people talking about Roth IRA in the USA, Stocks and Shares ISA in the UK, TFSA in Canada, and Super in Australia. These are types of accounts that allow you to earn profits on your investments, and you don't have to pay any taxes on them. So if you use the money inside these accounts to invest into index funds, all the profits will be yours because the government cannot take a cut.

One of the biggest questions when you first start is usually if you should invest all your money at the same time or do it gradually. This is something lots of investors argue about. Investing all your money as a lump sum is certainly more risky. However, if I'm investing in something I know will increase over time, like an S&P 500 index fund, then there is no point waiting. The longer you wait, the worse off, on average, you'll be. If you don't have the cash, don't wait to save up the money. Just start investing a fixed amount you can afford every month. Sometimes you're going to buy when the stocks are high, other times you're going to buy when the stocks are low, but overall this is going to balance out.

When you log on to an investing website or app, you'll see that there is something called ETFs, which are very similar to index funds, and a lot of people get confused. Both allow you to invest into a basket of stocks. However, the easy way to remember the difference is just to think of what ETF stands for: Exchange Traded Fund. If we break that down simply, it just means that it can be traded on the stock market throughout the day, whereas an index fund can only be bought and sold for a price that is set at the end of each trading day. You probably want to know which one is better. On average, if you're starting with little money, then ETFs may be a better option as they have lower minimum investment thresholds, and many brokers don't charge a trading commission.

If you are reading this and you're younger than 18 a way you can start investing under 18 is to open up a custodial account in the USA or a Junior Stocks and Shares ISA in the UK. To set up these accounts, you just need to ask your parents to do it for you. This information is not taught in schools, I wish I knew this when I was under 18. The real secret ingredient to the millionaire formula with index funds is time. And when you're younger, you have so much of it. That's because every year, as you keep adding to your investments, the interest starts to compound and grow at a rapid pace. It's a snowball effect. Once you reach a certain tipping point, the interest you're making is much more than the amount you're investing on a monthly basis. It's like when someone takes ages to get to a hundred thousand subscribers on YouTube, and then within a few months, they manage to hit the big million. The sooner you get started, the better, as time will be on your side.

When people talk about index funds, you will hear the S & P 500 again and again. People just love it. As I mentioned before, this is the top 500 public companies in the USA, but the cool thing is you don't actually have to be in the USA to invest in this. I'm in the UK, and it's one of my favourite investments. I just love to think that I own a small part of all the biggest companies in the USA.

Lots of people on the internet will tell you things like if you're able to invest 250 dollars per month with an 8% annual return over 42 years, you'll have over a million dollars in your account. Now, if you're able to invest that for another 10 years, you'll have over 2 million in your account. Of course, if you wanted to invest even more, then you're just going to speed up the whole process. This time frame puts people like myself off as I do not want to wait until I am 80 years old before I am a millionaire.

My Strategy with index funds

In 2019, I established a goal to generate an additional £100,000 every year by the time I turned 55, which is 15 years from 2019. Determining the required monthly investment to reach this target became one of my objectives, and I found compound interest calculators online to be invaluable for this purpose.

Based on my analysis outlined below, I discovered that by making a £7,000 deposit and contributing £200 monthly, I could potentially accumulate a lump sum of £100,000 after 15 years, assuming a 9% interest rate.

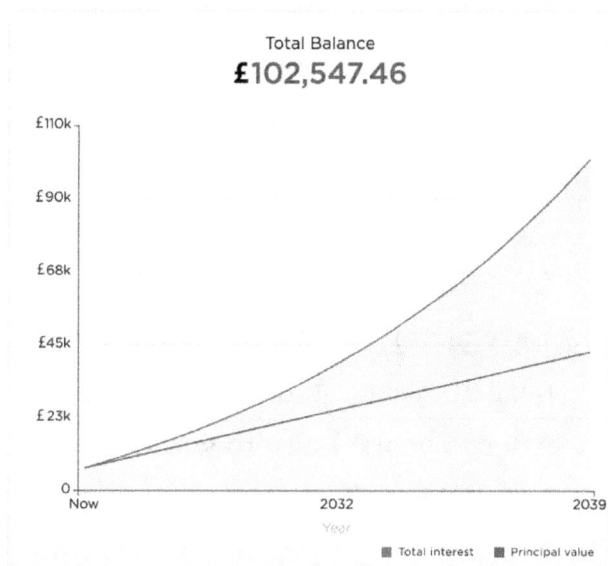

Three years ago, I began implementing this strategy, ensuring to invest in a new index fund at the beginning of each year. In 2020, 2021, and 2022, I initiated investments in three top index funds, each starting with a £7000 deposit, followed by £200 monthly contributions.

Investment Timeline

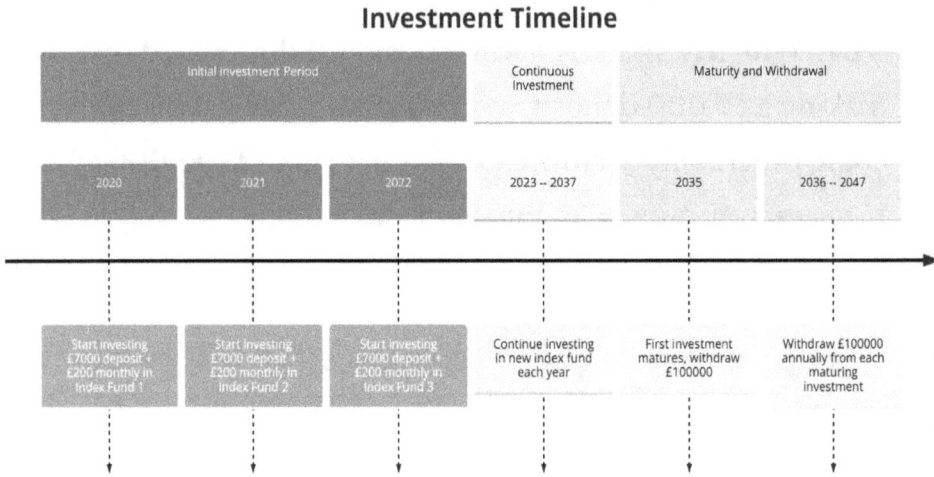

Initial Investment Period			Continuous Investment	Maturity and Withdrawal	
2020	2021	2022	2023 -- 2037	2035	2036 -- 2047
Start investing £7000 deposit + £200 monthly in Index Fund 1	Start investing £7000 deposit + £200 monthly in Index Fund 2	Start investing £7000 deposit + £200 monthly in Index Fund 3	Continue investing in new index fund each year	First investment matures, withdraw £100000	Withdraw £100000 annually from each maturing investment

My plan is to invest in a new index fund each year for the next 20 years, and then re-evaluate if I should continue. After 15 years, I aim to withdraw £100,000 annually. Since I started three years ago, my first investment will mature in 12 years time, that is in 2035. It's important to note that this strategy is tailored to my personal goals and may differ for others. To me, index funds are like virtual properties that will pay off in 15 years. One notable advantage is that index fund investments are highly liquid; I can take my money out whenever I want. In contrast, with property investing, selling a property involves a more time-consuming process, taking weeks or even months.

The 3 funds I am currently invested in are:

1- Fidelity 500 Index Fund (NASDAQMUTUALFUND:FXAI.X)

2- Schwab S&P 500 Index Fund (NASDAQMUTUALFUND:SWPP.X)

3- Vanguard 500 Index Fund Admiral Shares (NASDAQMUTUALFUND:VFIA.X)

These three major S&P 500 index funds are extremely similar in composition since each tracks the performance of the same index. All three are very low cost ways to invest in the 500 companies comprising the S&P 500 index.

INDEX OR FUND	1-YEAR TOTAL RETURN	3-YEAR ANNUALIZED RETURN	5-YEAR ANNUALIZED RETURN
S&P 500 INDEX	26.29%	10.00%	15.69%
VANGUARD 500 INDEX ADMIRAL SHARES	26.24%	9.96%	15.65%
SCHWAB S&P 500 INDEX FUND	26.25%	9.97%	15.66%
FIDELITY 500 INDEX FUND	26.29%	9.99%	15.68%
Data sources: Schwab, Fidelity, and Vanguard. Data as of Dec. 31, 2023.			

Notice from the table that the returns for the last three years have exceeded my anticipated 9%.

In my opinion, the key with index funds is not necessarily aiming to become a millionaire but reaching a comfortable goal. For instance, if you start with a £2,000 deposit and contribute £50 monthly to an index fund growing at 10% annually, you could have around £30,000 after 15 years, which is more than the current average wage in the UK.

Comparatively, spending £30,000 on a new car with a £1000 deposit and £685 monthly payments at 6.2% APR for 4 years seems like a waste of money to me. Instead, if you put a £1000 deposit into an index fund and contribute £685 monthly for 4 years, you could end up with over £40,000 at a 10% growth rate.

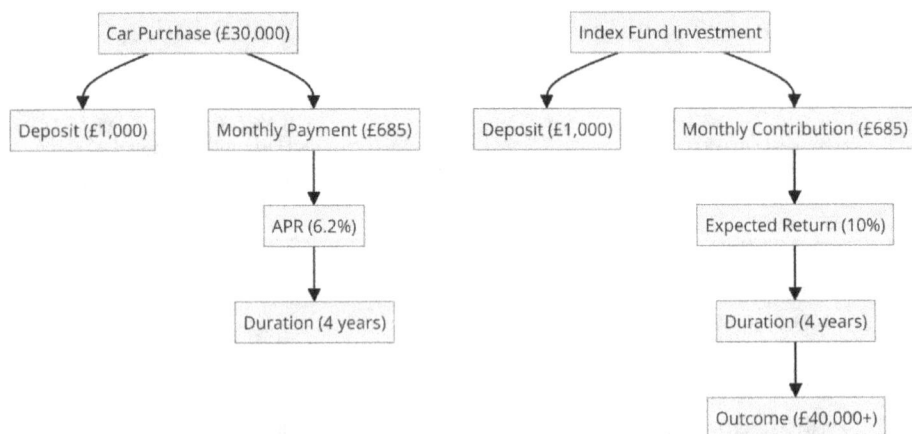

Car Purchase (£30,000)		Index Fund Investment	
Deposit (£1,000)	Monthly Payment (£685)	Deposit (£1,000)	Monthly Contribution (£685)
	APR (6.2%)		Expected Return (10%)
	Duration (4 years)		Duration (4 years)
			Outcome (£40,000+)

This is one reason why I opt for a used car – it allows me to invest the extra money into index funds. Index funds are versatile and can help you achieve both short-term and long-term goals. Usually, when credit lenders, like car loan companies, receive your deposit and monthly payments, they invest the money in index funds, often resulting in them making double the profit from your contributions.

Charles Schwab, Fidelity, and Vanguard

The brokerages that I love to use are Charles Schwab, Fidelity, and Vanguard. I call these the Big Three. The founder of Vanguard, John Bogle, is often referred to as the father of index fund investing. His Vanguard Group gave birth to index funds, so they're the oldest and most trusted. One thing to focus on when choosing a brokerage is the expense ratio, which is how much they are going to charge you per year. You obviously want to keep these as low as possible. Fidelity has the lowest costs, with a 0.015% expense ratio. Schwab's is only slightly higher at 0.02%, while the Vanguard 500 Index Fund Admiral Shares has a 0.04% expense ratio.

When you go to these brokerages you might be excited with the investment options available, for example they have different baskets of stocks some of which have been up more than 20% yearly for the past 10 years but if you are risk averse like me you should just stick to the major indices like S&P 500, FTSE 100 etc.

Another option is to consider investing in balanced funds. The concept behind these is to select the age you plan to retire, and Vanguard takes care of the rest by finding the appropriate mix of index funds for you. This could be a convenient choice if you prefer a hands-off approach to investing. However, I personally lean towards manual investing. Investing in a balanced fund is akin to driving an automatic car that handles everything for you, but it doesn't offer the same enjoyment as driving a stick shift.

Driving towards retirement

As a taxi driver, you enjoy the independence that comes with being your own boss, but with that freedom comes the responsibility of planning for your future. It's essential to think about retirement investments because you don't have the typical employer pension to fall back on. Simply investing £150 monthly in the S&P 500 index fund for 35 years with a 9% return can potentially yield at least £400,000. To put it in perspective, £150 is roughly what a taxi driver might spend on petrol in a week. If you opt for a more substantial investment, like £500 a month over 35 years, you could end up with around £1.5 million, making it a considerable sum for a comfortable retirement. That's the power of consistent investing and compound interest working in your favor, turning your hard earned money into a sizeable retirement fund as shown in the accompanying diagram.

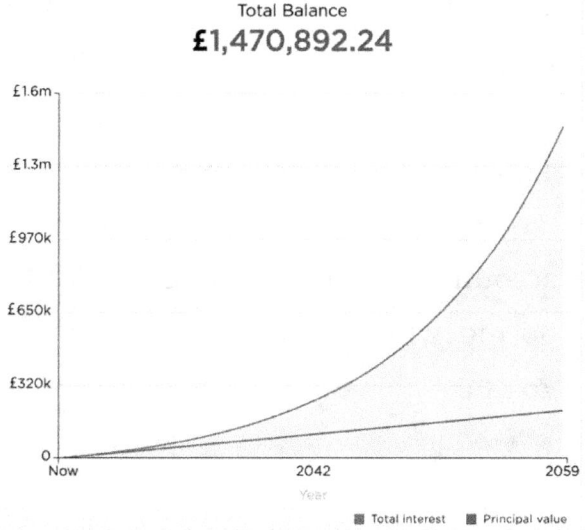

Investment details

Initial deposit

£0

Contribution amount

£500

Contribution frequency

| Monthly | Annually |

Years of growth

35 Years

Estimated rate of return

9%

Compound frequency

Monthly ▼

Total Balance
£1,470,892.24

£1.6m
£1.3m
£970k
£650k
£320k
0
Now   2042   2059

Year

■ Total interest   ■ Principal value

Achieving Short-Term Goals Through Smart Investing

You can also use index funds to reach your short-term goals. Take, for example, my recent cash purchase of a property at an auction for £50,000. To gather the needed funds, I started with a £7,000 deposit in the S&P 500 and added £1,000 each month for three years, reaching the target of £50,000. If the same amount sat in a savings account, it would only be about £43,000 after three years. So, index funds can be a practical way to achieve short-term goals.

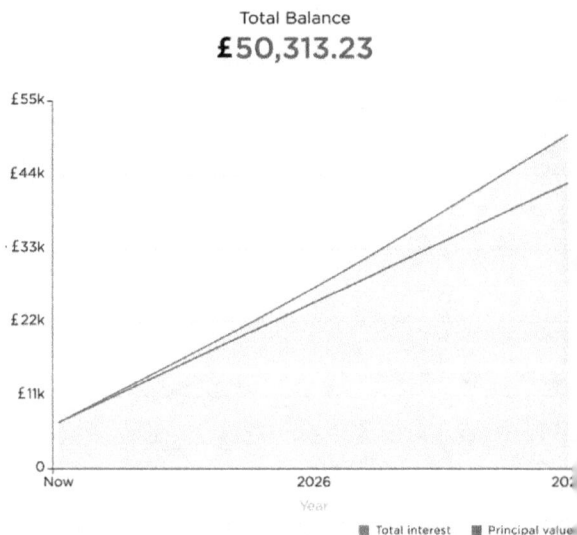

Chapter 10

Beyond the Impossible
Creating a Limitless Mind

Conquer in silence

There is this fictional philosophical debate on the meaning of life and what constitutes a life well lived. The debate is about a made-up chat between Napoleon Bonaparte, a famous leader known for fighting and conquering in Europe, and Buddha, a spiritual teacher known for seeking peace and wisdom through meditation. Napoleon tells Buddha that spending his life in silent meditation is a waste, while Buddha tells Napoleon that spending his life fighting and conquering is a waste. The story shows two very different views on what makes life valuable: one focuses on winning and power, and the other on finding inner peace and understanding life's deeper meaning. It's a way to think about what truly matters in life. For me personally I chose to be on both sides of the debate by conquering in silence.

Sometimes, you just need to step away from everything, take a break, and then make a comeback that surprises everyone. That's exactly what I decided to do – I went silent for 7 years. I refused to remain stuck where I was. Our society is filled with constant busyness, distractions, and noise, and sometimes the only way to bring about change is to disappear for a while. There's a saying that a person's public success is a result of their private efforts. Many people desire a higher level of fulfillment, but only a few are willing to eliminate distractions. Steve Jobs once wisely stated, "We do not talk about future products. We work on them in secret, and then we release them to the world."

I used to talk about success, made plans, and jotted things down. I invested in courses and books, but none of it seemed to be making a difference. That's when it hit me—I needed to take a break, put in the hard work in private, and then return to surprise everyone who doubted me.

There was a point when I even considered going without food, sleeping in my car, or crashing on friends' couches to save money, clear my debts, and eventually buy a house. I spent a few days bouncing around, trying to avoid bailiffs.

We celebrate athletes like Serena Williams, whose dominance in tennis came with overcoming societal barriers and injuries, and Michael Phelps, the most decorated Olympian, who battled personal struggles off the pool. Our admiration extends to critical thinkers and innovators such as Steve Jobs, whose journey with Apple Inc. was a rollercoaster of triumphs and setbacks, and Marie Curie, whose groundbreaking scientific discoveries were achieved amidst gender discrimination. Actors like Leonardo DiCaprio and Meryl Streep, too, are revered. DiCaprio's intense roles are the result of a career built from childhood, while Streep's path to becoming one of the greatest actresses involved overcoming early career criticism. We praise them and coin them our heroes, following them by the millions. We love what they do in public, but often, we don't know the story behind their glory. The blood, the hard work, the sweat, the tears they cried, the prayers they prayed, and the countless weeks they went without sleep to get where they are, remain unseen aspects of their inspiring journeys.

Our minds are similar to computers with limited memory; we can't overload them with every little thing. When we fill our minds with distractions, negative thoughts, and unproductive stuff, we leave less space and energy for the truly important things, like pursuing our dreams and achieving significant goals. Therefore, it's crucial that everything we think about or focus on is genuinely worth our time and energy. Often, it's necessary to assess everything and everyone around us and ask, "Is this worth my time and energy?" If it's not adding anything positive or helping us progress, it might be the right time to let it go and disconnect from it.

Once I had made the decision to put in the intense effort to pay off my debts and buy a house, I changed my approach. Instead of announcing my every move to everyone, I chose to disappear quietly and focus on the necessary work. This disappearing act required significant sacrifices in my relationships, friendships, and comfort. I encountered challenges, including criticism and moments of loneliness. Yet, these challenges served as tests of my commitment and desire to achieve my goal. The reward I currently enjoy far surpasses the difficulties I faced during that time.

Starting out as a taxi driver, you're bound to face tough times, what I like to call "test days." Adversity is something every taxi driver encounters now and then. What really counts is how you handle it. Facing life's challenges head-on, pushing through adversity, and getting the job done, especially when you don't feel like it, is crucial. There was a point when bailiffs were after me, and I felt completely alone with no help. That's when I realised it was time to stop making excuses and playing the blame game. I made the decision to stand up to life.

My journey has shown me that beyond intense suffering lies a whole new world that many people haven't explored. However, to reach that new world, you have to go through a lot of hard work. Some folks don't grasp the significance of facing hardships, and many fail to understand that it's okay to endure tough times.

Famous philosophers like Nietzsche, Gibran, and Helen Keller all kind of say something similar about life's tough times. Nietzsche basically says life is definitely full of struggles, but it's all about finding what those struggles mean to you. Gibran goes a bit further, saying the people who've really been through a lot end up being the strongest. And Helen Keller says, life has its tough moments, but we humans are pretty awesome at overcoming them. What they're getting at is this; hard times are a part of life, but they kind of shape us, make us stronger, and help us really value the good times.

Achieving freedom often involves taking risks and making sacrifices. It requires late nights, extra hours, persistence, and, most importantly, personal growth. If you don't transform into someone different, attaining freedom might be challenging. The person you are right now might not be equipped for the life you desire. To truly achieve it, you'll need to evolve into a different version of yourself. The transformation you undergo in the process is more crucial than the dream itself. The character you build, the courage you develop, and the faith you manifest are vital. Successful people can easily regain success even if they were to lose everything today because of the qualities they've developed.

To achieve success and bring your dream life to reality, it's crucial to set clear goals, devise an action plan, and maintain discipline to stick to your plan. Personally, I began with a goal of clearing my debts and then moved on to acquiring a house, and then the subsequent goals fell into place. Sustaining self-discipline requires a clear understanding of the goals you aim to achieve. It's essential to comprehend what success means to you. Without a clear direction or a roadmap to your goal, it's easy to lose your way or get sidetracked.

When setting goals, it's crucial to be clear and specific. Avoid vague goals like "I want to be rich in the next 5 years," as they lack clarity. Instead, opt for quantifiable goals. For instance, you can set a goal to save £24,000 in the current year. With this specific target, you can create a plan that makes sense for you. Breaking it down, you might aim to save £2,000 each month for the rest of the year, reaching your goal of £24,000 by year-end. Furthermore, you can dissect these goals to find strategies to save more or increase your income, making your objectives more achievable.

If you're aiming for your dream life, having self-discipline is crucial. It all begins with acknowledging your imperfections, no matter how small they may be. This might involve recognizing things like a less-than-ideal diet or habits that hinder productivity. Once you identify your weaknesses, you can make adjustments to minimise temptations. Personally, I decided to cut out social media and reduce news consumption. Additionally, I embraced a slow carb diet on weekdays and followed a keto diet on weekends, not just to boost my self-discipline but also to ensure I'm in optimal health to achieve my goals.

Self-discipline is a skill that can be learnt; you don't have to be born with it. Like any other skill, it demands practice and repetition. Just as your muscles get stronger and bigger with exercise, the same goes for self-discipline. When I began my job as a taxi driver, it took a few weeks for me to adapt to the long hours of driving. There were moments when I considered giving up, but remembering the draining nature of my previous job, I prioritised my mental health and carried on as a taxi driver.

Making changes takes time. Take building muscles, for example; it might take several weeks before you notice the results. Developing self-discipline requires a lot of focus and effort. Creating new habits is often necessary to boost self-discipline. It can be overwhelming, especially when concentrating on one goal at a time. To make it more manageable, keep it simple. Break down your big goal into smaller, doable steps. Instead of aiming for one big goal or trying to change all your habits, focus on just one thing each day to enhance your self-discipline. For improving fitness, you could exercise for 10 to 15 minutes every day. It's better to set smaller goals than attempting a 2-hour gym session every day. When I decided to pay off my debts, my goal was to consistently put £900 into my credit cards every week. Similarly, when I started getting into property investing, my initial target was to acquire just one house. So, my focus was on saving £1000 each week to accumulate £50,000 for my first property. Doing little things can make big things happen.

In life, it's oddly ironic that those who work the hardest, maintain strict discipline, and make sacrifices for their goals often end up the happiest. When you see a group of people gearing up for a distance race, don't pity or feel sorry for them. Instead, consider envying them. It may be hard to believe that giving up certain pleasures can result in profound happiness for those who haven't tested their self-discipline over an extended period. Choosing the challenging path in life can actually make it more manageable. People who willingly face challenges tend to be better equipped to handle unexpected difficulties. Additionally, foregoing certain pleasures like unhealthy food and excessive TV time can bring about significant improvements in overall well-being. It's not just about physical changes; it positively impacts self-esteem, lowers the risk of depression, and enhances body image.

Giving up pleasurable things such as spending money without control can also help you avoid crushing problems in the future. Today it might be inconvenient that you can't spend your entire salary, but tomorrow your savings can save you from bankruptcy or pay for an urgent medical intervention. Self-discipline is in itself a manifestation of your higher being and is connected with nobler strivings.

A human being, reduced to its primal form, has little ability for self-control. Operating in scarcity mode and left to its own devices, his primal brain will stuff his body until he won't be able to walk, it will eat everything it finds in the name of food, and it will assume that every step outside its comfort zone is a danger, and so he will never grow. Exerting self-control is working against the dominance of your primal brain. You forgo primal urges in order to reach bigger and more important goals or to cultivate values that are important to you.

You can live your life in a way that is congruent with who you are as a deeply complex human being, not a mere animal with the ability to reason. This leads to experiencing a wide variety of experiences that life has to offer, many of them are immensely more gratifying than merely satisfying the most basic human needs. Don't wait for tomorrow to do something you can do today. Have you been pondering starting on a new goal but are still procrastinating on it? The best course of action I find is to come up with the easiest, simplest, and quickest action you can take today to initiate momentum. If you are not feeling motivated to go to work as a taxi driver just decide you will go and take just one ride or 2 rides. Take it from there, step by step. When I started exercising regularly I decided I was going to do just 5 push ups each day. This has now turned into 30 minutes everyday for the past 8 years. I have now gone done to a healthy weight with my insulin resistance being a thing of the past. So the trick is to start small on any goal or task then you will get the momentum to continue.

If you want to start saving money, take just £1 out of your wallet and put it in a jar. Yes, it won't change anything today, but if you add £1 for the next 3 months, you would have saved almost £100 and you would have established the habit of saving. There's no excuse to not take simple actions now to get to your main goal. So break the chain of procrastination. Don't overthink it, and don't obsess over the future. Take care of establishing a tiny habit today and take it from there.

How to develop a limitless mindset

If you have seen the movie 'Limitless', you will wish that NZT was real. NZT a pill that could give you ultra-focus, motivation, and unleash your full potential. A way to become unstoppable and make your dreams a reality. The depressing truth is that NZT doesn't exist in real life and many people are stuck in a rut, constantly tired and unproductive. Time ticks by, the seasons keep changing, but they're left with a sinking feeling they're getting left behind. They have not achieved what they thought they would have by now. They tell themselves tomorrow will be different, but it never is. What if I told you becoming limitless is possible, not through some magical pill, but through a proven system that anyone can use. If you follow some simple steps I will explain next for just a few weeks, I am certain your life will radically change for the better and you will become limitless.

When I started working as a taxi driver in 2014, I found myself feeling totally drained of energy every day, constantly lethargic and tired, even after doing very little. And then I heard a stupidly simple sentence that changed my life completely: "You control your energy levels." Inside every single one of us is a person who wants to lay around all day eating junk food, doing nothing. But also inside every single one of us is someone extremely productive and ready to take on the world. Yet, as a society, we like to wait for this magical concept of motivation to switch us from one state to the other. But motivation is temporary. What's much more reliable is energy.

Imagine for a moment that you are powered by a battery, and the lower your charge gets, the worse you function and the harder everything is. If 100% was that limitless feeling and 0% was you about to fall asleep right now, what level is your energy at the moment? Stand up and shake your body for 10 seconds, and then clap. If you do this your energy levels will increase. The thing is, you never have to accept that low energy feeling. You can raise your energy levels and totally change your state of mind at any time. Most of us let our current state happen to us, rather than being proactive about changing it.

We all know things like exercise and eating healthier will raise our energy levels. In fact, if someone could put these things into a pill, it wouldn't be too far off the limitless pill. It is harder to do anything with low energy. So here's some of my easy ways to increase my energy levels really quickly:

1. I put on an upbeat energetic song that gets me psyched, and then dance around the room to it. Most often when I am at home before work I do the Maori Haka dance as performed by the All Blacks New Zealand Rugby team. I have done it countless times, so I'm familiar with all the lyrics.

2. I visualise myself scoring the winning goal at the World Cup and then physically celebrate like I actually just won the World Cup.

3. I do a 60-second workout. I usually do push-ups, burpees or jumping jacks, but it can be anything that gets my body moving and heart beating faster.

4. I blend a bunch of vegetables then drink it. It's like an energy drink but without the crash from the sugar.

5. I either walk fast on my treadmill for 5 minutes or do a quick 5-minute power yoga or stretching session with YouTube videos.

6. I eat raw nuts or seeds slowly, one at a time.

Obviously, you can come up with loads more of your own too as what raises energy for one person can be different for another. The crucial thing to do is to write down a list of about five different things that work for you, that will rapidly raise your energy levels whenever needed. It is good to write it down because you tend to forget when your energy levels are low. So Next time as soon as you catch your energy feeling low throughout the day, you can immediately do something on your energy list to raise your energy back up. And if you commit to doing this, you create a new baseline level where your natural default state is much more energetic. Which means you don't want to lay around doing nothing anymore. You're switched on and you're ready to crush whatever you need to do. But then, once you've got your energy list, you can move on to the next step.

One of the biggest benefits of the Limitless pill was the ability to get someone into a flow state, where he is in the zone with no distractions and work just feels effortless. The thing is, this flow state is completely real. You just need to use specific techniques to access it. So, alongside your energy list, you're now going to make a focus list, a checklist to follow as soon as you start work. And here are some things on mine:

Epic music

Get some noise-cancelling earbuds and put on a dramatic movie soundtrack on repeat. Because there are no lyrics, it's great for focus, but simultaneously makes you feel like you're working on something epic that might just save the world. My go-to is Hans Zimmer, pirates of the caribbean soundtrack or the champions league anthem. These can make me drive around for ages forgetting I am working.

I also like listening to documentaries on youtube about quantum physics. One of my best is the argument between Albert Einstein and Niels Bohr. Albert Einstein and Niels Bohr had a famous debate about how the universe works. Einstein believed that the universe had clear rules and that everything could be predicted if you had enough information. He didn't like the idea of randomness in quantum mechanics, famously saying, "God does not play dice with the universe." Bohr, on the other hand, argued that quantum mechanics shows the universe is not always predictable and that there's a fundamental uncertainty in the behaviour of tiny particles. The argument between them was about whether quantum mechanics could fully explain the behaviour of particles without clear, deterministic rules. Bohr defended quantum mechanics, which suggests that we can't predict exactly what will happen all the time at the quantum level.

So, who won? Most physicists today agree that Bohr's viewpoint was more accurate regarding quantum mechanics. The evidence gathered from experiments over the years supports the quantum mechanics theory, including its inherent randomness and uncertainty. This doesn't mean Einstein was wrong about everything; his theories of relativity are still fundamental to our understanding of the universe. But in this specific debate about quantum mechanics, Bohr is generally considered to have had the winning argument.

A cool thing I learned from quantum mechanics is that things might not happen if no one is watching. It's like if you don't keep an eye on your goals, they might not come true. So, if you set goals and keep checking on them, it's more likely they'll happen. It's as if by paying attention to your goals, you're helping steer them into becoming real, just like how observing something in quantum mechanics can affect its outcome.

Work blocks

This is quite literally the key to productivity. It's also called the Pomodoro Technique, and it's where you split your work into small tasks and work for 25 minutes straight, then have a five-minute break, and then repeat. Now, that may not sound like a revelation, but it works so well. Firstly, make sure you get an app on your phone because you need to be able to visibly see the timer counting down to give yourself that urgency and deadline. Secondly, the five-minute break means you don't burn yourself out and gives you time to do something from your energy lists, like grab a coffee. When I have low energy while working as a taxi driver I stop every 25 minutes and meditate for 5 minutes until my energy levels get up.

Kill time vampires

All of us have things that just drain our time and attention and completely take us out of that flow state. In fact, researchers found that there's something called attention residue, which means that even if you check your phone or emails for just a minute, when you go back to your work, some of your attention is still stuck on your phone or emails, which essentially just drains your productivity. The solution is brutal but necessary. In my case, once I get home during the intervals between my shifts as a taxi driver, I activate the Do Not Disturb mode on my phone. And if there's anything else that could disrupt my flow, I find a way to block it. I guarantee you will get into that deep work state more often, where you really do feel limitless if you find a way to *kill time vampires*.

What is your ultimate goal?

While you work you need to ask yourself the big question: What do you want to achieve? What is your ultimate goal? Is it making a specific amount of money? What is the one thing you want to achieve the most? Because if you don't have an ultimate goal, it's so easy to just drift through life because there's no purpose or need to work hard.

Here's the secret that most people miss. You need to attach an emotional reason for your goal. Let's say your ultimate goal is to make a million dollars. That's great, but go to a deeper level by asking why. Maybe you want to make a million dollars so you can give your parents the life they deserve while they're still alive. Or you just don't have to constantly worry about money anymore. Or maybe you want that feeling of freedom and not having to endlessly work a job you hate. I guarantee that getting really honest with yourself about the deeper 'why' behind the goal is what is going to keep you going when motivation drops and things get tough. Not a day should go by where you don't think about your ultimate goal and that visual image of why you're doing it because that's what will get you up in the mornings and keep you going. My first goal was freedom from my soul draining office job then the next goal was to clear my debts then the next was to buy a house. Then I discovered a way to gain financial freedom, I made it my ultimate quest and pursued it with all my might.

The Pareto Principle

So, what is the system to actually achieve this ultimate goal? There's a crucial concept that separates people who are simply productive from the ultra-successful people who genuinely seem limitless. The Pareto Principle states that roughly eighty percent of your results will come from twenty percent of your actions. In other words, a small number of things really matter, and the rest don't. If you're going to achieve your ultimate goal, you need to create a focus list by identifying which things contribute the most to your goals and either eliminate or delegate the rest. For example, if you're trying to make more money, what are the 20% of things that are vital? Is it checking your email every 20 minutes, or getting on the phone to close sales? To reach that limitless state, you should be focused on fewer things, but the things that have the largest return on investment (ROI). The one thing that had the largest ROI for me was being online on the Uber app accepting ride requests. So, everything else that I did each day was geared towards making sure I got online on time.

Feeling limitless is about working smarter and on the really important things that move you to your ultimate goal the fastest. And looking at your daily activities and habits through the lens of the Pareto Principle is the easiest way to predict your future. If you find a lot of things that don't move you significantly closer to your ultimate goal, eliminate or delegate.

So, in summary create an energy and a focus list, then fill your days with the tasks that move you closest to your ultimate goal. But if you're sitting there right now, frustrated, thinking you kind of knew all of this anyway, you're right. This isn't a secret. It's really simple to totally transform your life and get the things you want. But simple doesn't mean easy. It means sacrifice.

The Seinfeld Strategy

In the Limitless movie, Eddie becomes wealthy, powerful, influential, successful, but he sacrifices his old life of relaxing, drinking, and chilling out. The real question is, are you willing to make that short-term sacrifice for your ultimate goal? If you're not, that's fine. Not everyone needs to be living some ultra-productive life to be happy. But if you have big dreams, here's what you do right now:

Get a blank sheet of paper and draw 30 boxes. This represents the next 30 days of your life. At the top of the paper, write down your ultimate goal. In one corner, rewrite your energy list, and in the other, your focus list. Finally, pin this paper to your wall in a place you will constantly see. Now, for the next 30 days try these three simple steps. Whenever your energy isn't high, you're going to do something from your energy list. Whenever you're working, you're going to use the things on your focus list. And whenever you're deciding what to do each day, you're going to pick the tasks that contribute most to hitting your ultimate goal. And at the end of each day, you get to put a big X in the box if you did all three. If you didn't, then you have to leave that box blank. This is often called the Seinfeld Strategy, as Jerry Seinfeld used this to build the habit of writing at least one joke every single day. But you can use it for any habit because essentially it builds up a momentum streak where you don't want to break the chain of crosses. And before you know it, you've built a habit, and that's what will happen here as well. If you can commit to just 30 days of these three steps, before you know it, you will naturally be using these techniques without having to think about it. Or, in other words, you will be well on your way to feeling limitless.

My daily target was to generate a minimum of £180, and I would mark an X when I achieved this goal. Implementing these straightforward strategies enabled me to transition from a £28,000 debt to earning over £20,000 monthly. I struggle to see how I could have done this in any other job.

Conclusion

As you conclude your reading journey with this book, I genuinely hope that the insights and guidance within its chapters have proven to be not just informative, but transformative for you. If this literary journey has indeed been a source of assistance, I am confident that your path to success, whether it be within the taxi business or any endeavor you choose will be illuminated by the principles shared in these pages. By embracing the schedule and motivation techniques outlined here, I believe you are not merely equipped but empowered to navigate the challenges that lie ahead.

Hope you can use the wisdom from this book to fuel your efforts and reach achievements you might not even have thought possible. Remember, success isn't just a goal you reach; it's a journey that takes hard work and determination.

It's crucial to embrace the principle of abundance, acknowledging that there's an abundance of good things, happiness, opportunities, and resources for everyone. Let go of the notion that someone else's success takes away from your own. Cultivate a mindset that fosters gratitude, generosity, and a positive perspective on life.

To wrap it up, I wish you the very best in everything you do. Good luck not only in your taxi business but in every part of your life. May your days be filled with successes, your nights with happiness, and your journey decorated with the sweet rewards of your well-deserved success.

About the Author

Charles West's journey from the confines of a finance office in London to the freedom of the roads is nothing short of inspiring. Charles grew up in London where he honed his analytical skills and earned a Master's degree in Accountancy and Finance from Birmingham City University. However, despite his academic achievements and a promising career in finance, he felt trapped and unfulfilled.

Working in finance in London, he found himself drowning in debt and struggling to make ends meet despite earning a decent salary. But a dramatic shift occurred when he made the bold decision to become a taxi driver—a move that many might have found unusual, but for Charles, it was the gateway to a new and exhilarating phase of life.

Through his website, www.mdcabbie.com, Charles shares the experiences, insights, and lessons from his incredible journey. His transition from a finance professional to a successful taxi driver, and eventually to a savvy property investor and index fund enthusiast, is a testament to his resilience, creativity, and entrepreneurial spirit.

Charles's story is not merely a narrative of personal success; it serves as a guide to finding fulfillment and financial freedom by following one's passions and seizing opportunities. His remarkable journey from being £28,000 in debt to building a property portfolio worth over £1 million in less than eight years illustrates how anyone, with perseverance and determination, can overcome challenges and realise their dreams.

References

Dweck, C. S. (2006). Mindset: The New Psychology of Success. Random House.

Tolle, E. (1997). The Power of Now: A Guide to Spiritual Enlightenment. New World Library.

Covey, S. R. (1989). The 7 Habits of Highly Effective People: Powerful Lessons in Personal Change. Free Press.

Ferriss, T. (2007). The 4-Hour Workweek: Escape 9-5, Live Anywhere, and Join the New Rich. Harmony.

Ferriss, T. (2010). The 4-Hour Body: An Uncommon Guide to Rapid Fat-Loss, Incredible Sex, and Becoming Superhuman. Crown Archetype.

Cirillo, F. (2018). The Pomodoro Technique. Currency.

Nietzsche, F. (1889). Thus Spoke Zarathustra. Random House.

Gibran, K. (1923). The Prophet. Alfred A. Knopf.

Keller, H. (1903). The Story of My Life. Doubleday, Page & Company.

Sykes, T. (2011). Penny Stocks: How to Trade and Invest in Penny Stocks. CreateSpace Independent Publishing Platform.

Hagstrom, R. G. (1994). The Warren Buffett Way. John Wiley & Sons.

David Greene. (2019). "BRRRR: Buy, Rehab, Rent, Refinance, Repeat: The Ultimate BRRRR Strategy Guide to Get Long-Term Rentals and Build Wealth." BiggerPockets Publishing.

Rob Dix and Rob Bence. (2016). "Property Investment For Beginners: A Property Geek guide." Rethink Press Limited.

Dave Ramsey. (2011). "The Total Money Makeover: A Proven Plan for Financial Fitness." Thomas Nelson.

Housel, M. (2020). The Psychology of Money: Timeless Lessons on Wealth, Greed, and Happiness. Harriman House Ltd.

Kiyosaki, R. T. (1997). Rich Dad Poor Dad: What the Rich Teach Their Kids About Money That the Poor and Middle Class Do Not! Warner Books.

www.ingramcontent.com/pod-product-compliance
Lightning Source LLC
LaVergne TN
LVHW052025080426
835513LV00018B/2155